Peak District

central area

Ian Johnson

This book is dedicated to my father,
Alan Johnson (1929 - 2006)
who showed me the way,
and guides me still.

Scenic Walks
in the
Peak District
central area

30 circular walks from $2\frac{1}{2}$ to $6\frac{3}{4}$ miles
Accurate route maps
Detailed instructions
Starting point maps
Elevation profiles

Ian Johnson
Johnson Publishing

Published by;
Johnson Publishing
160 Sutton Road
Mansfield
Notts NG18 5HH
email: johnson.publishing@virgin.net
website: www.johnsonpublishing.co.uk

Published 2010

Text© Ian Johnson
Maps© Ian Johnson
Line illustrations© Cliff Rowbotham

All route maps are based on 1940's Ordnance Survey Provisional Edition 1:25000 maps and revised from field surveys made by Johnson Publishing in 2009. The maps on pages 14 to 24 are based on Bartholomew's map of the Peak District 1935, updated by Johnson Publishing in 2009. Every effort has been made to ensure that the information given in this book is accurate. The publisher accepts no responsibility for any loss, injury or inconvenience caused by anyone whilst using this book.

ISBN 978-0-95425-747-7

Printed by Linney Group, Mansfield, Nottinghamshire

Contents

Acknowledgments

Thanks to the following family and friends; Margaret (my mother), Anne, Marj, Rod, John and Alan, experienced walkers who walked the routes and meticulously checked the instructions. Thanks to Cliff Rowbotham for the line drawings. Thanks also to the information given by the staff at The Peak District National Park Authority. However any errors of any kind are of course the responsibility of the author.

Introduction

The Peak District National Park is approximately thirty nine miles by twenty four miles, at its extremities. It has a great variety of scenery, from vast moorlands to spectacular limestone dales and meadows. These two contrasting types of landscape are often referred to as the Dark Peak and White Peak. The underlying rock of the Dark Peak is gritstone, whilst the White Peak is limestone. The former is largely to the northern and eastern edges of the Peak District, whilst the latter forms the central and southern areas.

This guidebook includes both types of landscape, however the majority of the walks are in the White Peak. Although I have called the book 'Scenic Walks in the Peak District - central area', there are no formally recognised boundaries as to what constitutes the central, northern, western, eastern or southern areas of the Peak District. The area I have chosen to call the 'central' area is based on my preference, rather than geographical accuracy.

The area I have used for the thirty walks is approximately twelve by twelve miles. The northern boundary being the Longshaw Estate, the southern limit is the village of Elton, just to the south of Robin Hood's Stride. To the east the boundary is Birchen Edge to the east of Baslow, with the most westerly walk being in Chee Dale to the east of Buxton. Within this small area is an impressive variety of scenery. To the north is the moorland and steep-sided valleys of the Bretton Clough area. To the east is the almost unbroken line of gritstone of Froggatt Edge, Curbar Edge and Baslow Edge. In the central and western areas, the limestone plateau is incised with the spectacular limestone dales of Monsal Dale, Lathkill Dale, and Chee Dale. The popular destinations of Chatsworth Park and Bakewell also lie within this compact but diverse area.

Locations of the walks

Rather than the walks being dotted around more or less evenly, the routes cover what I consider to be the most scenic areas. Therefore some of the routes may adjoin each other and there are several walks where the routes partly overlap. For example, Walks 18

Introduction

and 20 both include Froggatt and Curbar Edges. As these gritstone edges give some of the best views in the Peak District, hopefully it won't be a hardship. Sometimes two or three walks start from the same spot, making it easier to combine a couple of walks in one day.

Starting Points

All the walks begin from a convenient parking area, either a car park, roadside parking or a lay-by. On pages 18 to 24, I have included detailed road maps and instructions to help you find the parking areas. I have given grid references to help locate the points. (Abbreviated to GR in the text). Information on reading grid references is given on OS Explorer maps. Where a walk starts from roadside parking in a village, it doesn't interfere with residents' parking. Several of the walks start from car parks run by the Peak District National Park Authority. For an annual permit, ring 01629 816211 or email: parking.permits@peakdistrict.gov.uk.

Public Transport

Many of the walks are accessible by bus. There is a 'Peak District Bus Timetable' published in book form twice a year. Available from Tourist Information Centres. More public transport information is available at www.peakdistrict.gov.uk.

The Walk Routes

All walks are circular and each walk has a route map with directions on the facing page. Some walks are better at certain times of the year, for example, the Edge walks are particularly good in August and September when the heather is flowering. Where this is the case, I mention it in the 'Summary of the Walk' section. I have tried to keep road walking to an absolute minimum. Of course it is sometimes unavoidable when linking paths together. It is obvious from my maps where the route uses a road, as it is indicated in dots. Normally the road sections are in towns or villages, or on country lanes. Where a main road has to be used there is normally a pavement. Even quiet lanes can be dangerous, so take extra care on roads and at road crossings.

For each walk I have given an objective summary of the walk, and have included a heading - 'Disadvantages'. Even in the glorious Peak District the entire length of every walk cannot be perfect. For instance I have indicated if a walk has a lot of step-stiles, a rocky section, a steep climb or descent etc. This may be of help to you in deciding which walks to do.

Stiles

Stiles are basically of two types; 'squeeze stiles' and 'step-stiles'. The names are self explanatory, the former are also called 'gap stiles'. In the 'directions' text, where a path includes a squeeze stile it will state 'go through a stile', where it is a step-stile it will be 'go over a stile'. Thankfully for dog owners and people with hip problems, there seems to be a shift away from step-stiles in favour of a gated opening or a gap stile.

Rights of Way

The majority of the routes use public footpaths and public bridle-ways. Some routes use concessionary paths, this is where the landowner allows the public to use a route, without it being legally designated as a right of way. One such route in this book is the section following the River Wye, between the former Cressbrook and Litton mills. Some of the routes in Chatsworth Park also use concessionary paths.

An attractive feature of some of the walks is the use of so-called 'green lanes'. They are walled tracks winding alongside fields. In the walk directions if they are narrow, I tend to refer to them as walled tracks. If wide enough for a vehicle, I call them green lanes.

Parts of several walks use paths on Open Access land. This is land where walkers have access to an area as designated in the Countryside and Rights of Way Act 2000. Some walks use sections of the Monsal Trail, most of which runs along a disused rail line. (The Midland Line between London and Manchester, closed

Introduction

in 1968). Some paths don't fall into any of the above types. They are simply paths or tracks that are in free and general use.

Most path signage uses the standard colour-coded arrows; yellow for public footpaths, blue for public bridleways and white for concessionary paths.

Distances

The distances given for the walks have been obtained by using a hand-held GPS navigation unit. They are given in miles, with kilometres in brackets. Distances have been rounded up or down to the nearest $1/4$ mile.

Walking Times

The times given for each walk are for guidance only. They allow time for short breaks and for enjoying the views etc. It is always better to err on the side of caution and allow yourself too much time rather than too little. As a guide, I consider that $2\,1/2$ - 3 miles per hour average walking speed, is about right. Of course everyone has their own idea of what is a comfortable walking speed. You will have to use judgement and adjust the times accordingly.

Gradients

As is the case when measuring from a map, the distances do not take into account the extra distance walked by going up or down hills. A 30° slope adds an extra 15%, whilst for 45° it increases to 41% extra. However as the average angle of even the steepest slopes on the walks in this book is only about 30°, the extra distances aren't that significant.

Elevation Profile Graphs

On pages 86 to 89, I have plotted gradient profiles for the walks. They axis of the graphs are height in feet against miles. They are provided as a means of comparing the hills between walks. They and are subject to slight errors. Don't be confused into thinking that the gradients of the plots represent the actual gradients of the hills. The scale means they appear far steeper than they are.

Grading of the walks

It is always difficult to give walks a grading. There is no official system. I have attempted to grade the walks and have given them the following grades - Easy, Moderate and Difficult. The gradings are based only on the walks in this book. Therefore the walks graded as 'difficult' are only difficult compared to the other walks. The gradings are based mainly on the difficulty or otherwise of the paths and the steepness and number of hills. Of course the weather can play a part too, a walk that is easy in dry conditions may be more difficult in wet weather. It is far from scientific. The gradings are as follows:

Easy - Good paths with little or no rocky or muddy sections. Only gentle hills with little ascent.

Moderate - Generally good paths, but some rocky sections. One or two steep sections.

Difficult - Significant sections of rocky paths. Several steep sections of significant ascent, or descent.

Heights

The maximum height attained on each walk is given on the map page and obtained from the OS map. The figure for the total ascent is derived from the elevation profile graphs. It is intended for reference and as a comparison between walks only, as it may be subject to error.

Refreshments

Where a café or pub is mentioned, this is not necessarily meant to be a recommendation of the establishment.

Walking with dogs

Keep dogs under control at all times and on a lead near livestock. On moorland areas dogs should be on a lead at all times, as sheep are present all year round and dogs can cause disturbance to ground-nesting birds in the spring.

Introduction

The Route Directions

All the directions in this book have been compiled with great care. They have been double-checked by a group of friends who have walked all the routes and who have many years' experience of walking in the Peak District. However if any errors remain, they are entirely my responsibility.

The numbers on the map cross-reference with the corresponding numbered instructions on the page opposite. This helps you to keep track of where you are on the map at each of the numbered instructions. If you think you have gone wrong, it is best to retrace your steps until you regain a recognisable part of the correct route. The walk directions are on the facing page to the map, to save having to change pages on the walk. Any distances over 400 yards are normally given in fractions of a mile. The following conversion table may be useful as a guide -

> 100 yards - 91.5 metres
> 1/4 mile - 440 yards (402 metres)
> 1/3 mile - 582 yards (531 metres)
> 1/2 mile - 880 yards (805 metres)
> 3/4 mile - 1320 yards (1207 metres)
> 1 mile - 1760 yards (1609 metres) (1 km - 0.62 mile)

The Maps

Each walk has a route map facing the walk directions page. See the key to symbols used on page 16. All maps have north pointing to the top of the page. The scale of each map is shown along the bottom edge. The heights are shown in feet and the contour lines are at 25 feet intervals. Whilst it is not essential to carry an Ordnance Survey map with you on the walks, it may help you if you go astray, (hopefully unlikely). It may also contribute to your enjoyment of the walk. All the walks fall within the OS. OL24 Explorer, The Peak District - White Peak Area (1:25,000). For an overview of the whole Peak District use the Touring Map 4, Peak District (1:63360).

Safety on the hills

I would advise walkers to wear comfortable walking boots (or at least trail shoes). Even at the relatively low altitudes of the walks in this guide the weather can change quickly, at any time of year. Therefore take additional layers of clothing and waterproofs. In summer you may need a sunhat, suncream and insect repellent. An adequate amount of food and drink should also be carried. You may also wish to carry a sit-mat. A map, whistle and compass are also advisable. However so much of what people take and don't take is down to personal preferences and experience. Don't weigh yourself down.

Mountain Rescue

Mountain rescue is co-ordinated by the police. If you need assistance dial 999. Be aware that you cannot rely on mobile phone reception in some areas of the Peak District.

Changes over time

During the life of this book some of the instructions may be rendered incorrect by changes to gates or stiles, the removal or addition of walls and fences, house building etc. I hope to reprint the guide with updated information at intervals.

Finally

The total mileage of the walks in this guide is 143 miles (230 kilometres). You could do them all in a couple of weeks, or a couple of years. However long it takes, I hope you enjoy them, as we have done in the planning of the book.

The Peak District National Park and surrounding area

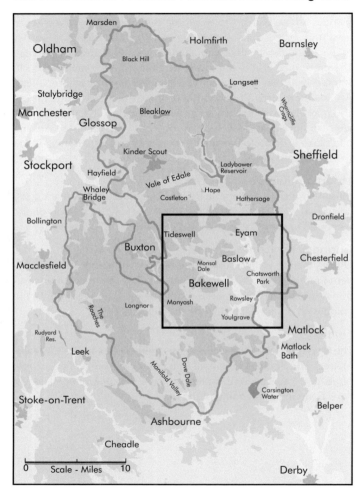

National Park boundary

Enlargement of inset on map opposite - central area

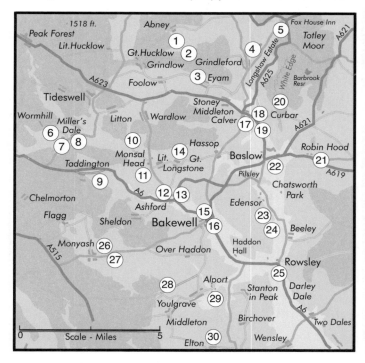

Key to map above and on opposite page -

Heights -

Sea level to 250 feet	
250 to 500 feet	
500 to 1000 feet	
1000 to 2000 feet	
Above 2000 feet	

(1) Approximate location of walk

Roads classified as 'A' roads

Roads classified as 'B' roads

Unclassified roads

Key to the walking route maps

━ ━ ━ ━ ━ Walking route

• • • • • • • • • • • Walking route - road sections

- - - - - - - Other paths, not on the route

================ Main roads

============ Minor roads

P Designated parking area

② Location of corresponding route instruction

⟶ Indicated direction in which to walk

N
↑
✝ Direction of north

———————— Field boundary

Contour lines (25 feet intervals)

Buildings and built-up areas

Rocks and rock features

Lake or pond

River or stream

1124 △ Triangulation Pillar - height shown in feet.
(White concrete pillars - abbreviated to 'trig. point').

♱ ♦ ✝ Place of worship

Open Access area

PH Public House

Walks List

Starting point locater map for walks 1-5

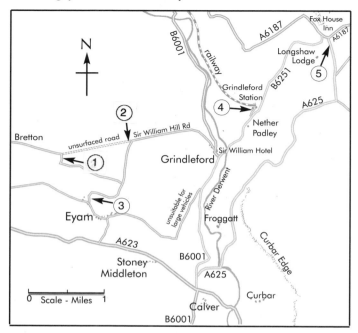

Directions to parking locations and relevant information

Walk	Title (abbreviated)	Starting Point:	Grid reference	Page
1	Bretton Clough	Sir William Hill Road	SK 2245 7803	26

Directions: From the A623 (from the Baslow direction) turn right at Calver crossroads, signed 'Froggatt, Sheffield A625'. At Grindleford, in 1³/₄ miles, turn sharp left signed 'Hathersage B6001'. The road rises and bends right, with the Sir William Hotel on the right. Turn sharp left opposite the hotel, onto the steeply climbing Sir William Hill Road. After 1¹/₄ miles the road bends sharply to the left. At the bend, Sir William Hill Road continues straight on, as an unsurfaced 'Byway'. Turn right onto this wide gravelly road, and park on either verge, near the junction.

Erratum - the directions to the start of Walk 1 lead you to the start of Walk 2 and vice-versa

Directions to parking locations and relevant information

Walk	Title	Starting Point:	Grid reference	Page
2	Eyam Moor	Sir William Hill Road	SK 2102 7775	28

Directions: From the A623 (from the Baslow direction) turn right at Calver crossroads, signed 'Froggatt, Sheffield A625'. At Grindleford in 1³/₄ miles turn sharp left, signed 'Hathersage B6001'. The road rises and bends right, with the Sir William Hotel on the right. Turn sharp left opposite the Hotel, onto the steeply climbing Sir William Hill Road. After 1¹/₄ miles the road bends sharply to the left. Keep on the road and turn right in ¹/₂ mile, signed 'Great Hucklow, Bretton'. In 1 mile the road bends sharp left. Park on the right-hand side grass area just before the bend.

Walk	Title (abbreviated)	Starting Point:	Grid reference	Page
3	Eyam & Riley Gr.	Eyam, car park	SK 2164 7675	30

Directions: From Stoney Middleton, keep on the A623 for ³/₄ mile then turn right signed 'Eyam B6251'. At the top of the hill bear left. Drive through Eyam past the church and Eyam Hall. A little further on, turn right up Hawkhill Road at the car park sign. There is a choice of two public car parks, both on the right-hand side of the road. The pay-and-display one, where the public toilets are, or a free car park kindly provided by Eyam Parish Council. This car park is just beyond the pay-and-display one. Be aware that it has the following closing times;
April to Sep-8 pm. Oct to March-5 pm. (The grid reference given is for the free car park).

Walk	Title	Starting Point	Grid Reference	Page
4	Padley Gorge	Grindleford Station	SK 2510 7870	32

Directions: As for Walk 2 to Grindleford, then keep on the B6251. Go over Grindleford Bridge and in ¹/₂ mile, turn left just after the Maynard Arms, signed Grindleford Station. Park anywhere on the left-hand side of this lane. Free parking. (Don't park in the little private parking area near the café, on the right-hand side).

Walk	Title	Starting Point	Grid Reference	Page
5	Longshaw Estate	Longshaw Estate - Woodcroft car park	SK 2665 8006	34

Directions: From the A623 at Calver, turn right onto the A625. In about 100 yards turn right, signed 'Froggatt, Sheffield A625'. In 1¹/₂ miles turn left at the junction with the B6054. Keep straight on, ignoring the road leaving to the right. The Woodcroft, National Trust car park is signed to the left, about 150 yards before the junction with the A6187.
Pay-and-display (free for National Trust members).

Starting point locater map for walks 6-13

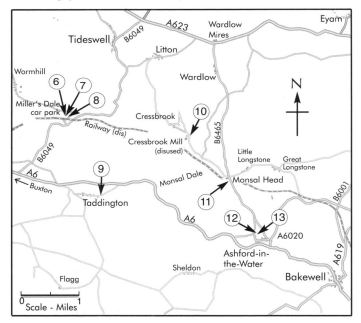

Directions to parking locations and relevant information

Walk	Title	Starting Point:	Grid reference	Page
6	Chee Dale	Miller's Dale car park	SK 13907330	36
7	Monk's Dale	Miller's Dale car park	SK 13907330	38
8	Tideswell Dale	Miller's Dale car park	SK 13907330	40

Directions: From the A6, take the turning onto the B6049, signed to Tideswell. (If coming from Bakewell, the turn is 5 1/2 miles on the right. From Buxton it is 3 3/4 miles). In about 1 1/4 miles, after descending into the dale, turn left signed 'Wormhill, P'. Go up the hill, under a bridge and the car park entrance is on the left. Pay-and-display. Toilets. Provided by the Peak District National Park Authority.

Directions to parking locations and relevant information

Walk	Title	Starting Point:	Grid reference	Page
9	Taddington Moor	Taddington, roadside	SK 14767103	42

Directions: If coming from Bakewell on the A6, turn left (after 3³/₄ miles) at the road signed 'Taddington, Queen's Arms'. (This is just after the road becomes a dual carriageway). On entering the village, the road bends sharp right and widens. There are grass verges on either side. After passing a street named Townend on the left, park along the right-hand side verge, adjacent to a field.

If coming from Buxton, turn right (after 6 miles) signed 'Taddington village'. Go through the village. At the end of the village after passing the pub on the left and the Memorial Institute on the right, park on the left-hand verge adjacent to a field, where the road is wide.

Walk	Title	Starting Point	Grid Reference	Page
10	Cressbrook Dale	Cressbrook, near mill	SK 17377275	44

Directions: From the A6, take the turning onto the A6020, (1¹/₂ miles from Bakewell, 7¹/₂ miles from Buxton) signed 'Chesterfield, Sheffield'. Take the first turn left, signed 'B6465 Monsal Head, Wardlow', into Ashford-in-the-Water. In a few yards, turn right, signed 'Monsal Head, Wardlow' (still the B6465). Go up the hill for a mile. Just after the road to the right (to Little Longstone) turn left. Pass the café at Monsal Head and go down the steep hill. Then ignore the road to the right and the little car park on the left. In half a mile, there is ample roadside parking adjacent to the former Cressbrook Mill.

Walk	Title	Starting Point	Grid Reference	Page
11	Miller's Dale	Monsal Head car park	SK 18527148	46

Directions: As above, but turn left just before Monsal Head into the long stay public car park. (It is just before the road to the right, signed Little Longstone). Pay-and-display. Public toilets. (Also roadside parking on the Little Longstone road).

Walk	Title	Starting Point	Grid Reference	Page
12	Magpie Mine	Ashford-in-the-Water	SK 19486975	48
13	Monsal Dale	Ashford-in-the-Water	SK 19486975	50

Directions: As for Walk 9, into Ashford-in-the-Water, but instead of turning right to Monsal Head, keep straight on through the village. The road bends right, along Fennel Street. The car park is just off the road, signed to the right, in about 150 yards. Free parking. Public toilets.

Starting point locater map for walks 14-22

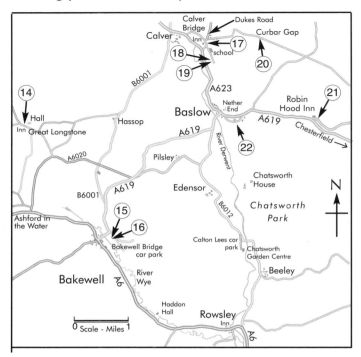

Directions to parking locations and relevant information

Walk	Title (abbreviated)	Starting Point:	Grid reference	Page
14	Great Longstone	Great Longstone	SK 19807190	52

Directions: From the A6 Matlock direction: In Bakewell turn right at the roundabout (onto the A619) towards Baslow. In $3/4$ mile turn left onto the B6001, signed 'Hathersage'. At the roundabout turn left on the A6020, signed 'Ashford A6020, Buxton (A6)'. In $3/4$ mile at a left-hand bend, turn right signed 'Great Longstone'. Keep on the main road and in $1/2$ mile enter Great Longstone village. At the second pub on the left (The Crispin Inn), park along the section of road opposite and slightly beyond. Take care not to restrict access to gateways.

Directions to parking locations and relevant information

Walk	Title (abbreviated)	Starting Point:	Grid reference	Page
15	Monsal Trail	Bakewell Bridge	SK 22056865	54
16	Haddon Hall	Bakewell Bridge	SK 22056865	56

Directions: From the A6 Matlock direction. At the roundabout in Bakewell by the Rutland Hotel, turn right onto the A619, (not currently signed). Go through the town, over the bridge and immediately turn right along Station Road. In a few yards bear right onto Coombs Road and then right into Bakewell Bridge car park. Pay-and-display.

Walk	Title (abbreviated)	Starting Point	Grid Reference	Page
17	Baslow Edge	Calver Bridge	SK24737435	58
18	Froggatt Edge	Calver Bridge	SK24737435	60
19	Bramley Wood	Calver Bridge	SK24737435	62

Directions: Calver Bridge is the area named after the original bridge, which is now bypassed by the A625. It is about 800 yards south-east of the crossroads at Calver and 1^1/2 miles north of Baslow. Turn off the A625 by the Bridge Inn, signed Curbar. There are several parking sites. Either turn first right and park on the service road away from the school, towards the top end. Or park along the road, before or after the bridge. (On the right-hand side, before the bridge). There is also some parking on the left-hand side of Dukes Road, the road diagonally left, opposite the pub.

Walk	Title (abbreviated)	Starting Point	Grid Reference	Page
20	White Edge	Curbar Gap car park	SK 26257470	64

Directions: Turn off the A623 as above, then turn right up the hill, signed Curbar. Go through the village, continuing up the hill. The car park is a further ^{1}/2 mile, just over the brow of the hill on the left. Pay-and-display. Provided by the Peak District National Park Authority.

Walk	Title (abbreviated)	Starting Point	Grid Reference	Page
21	Birchen Edge	Birchen Edge car pk.	SK 28107210	66

Directions: The area known as Robin Hood is off the A619, 5 miles west of Chesterfield and a mile east of Baslow. Turn onto the B6050, signed Cutthorpe, Whittington'. (Sign not visible from Chesterfield direction). The public car park is just beyond the entrance to the Robin Hood Inn. Free.

Walk	Title (abbreviated)	Starting Point	Grid Reference	Page
22	Chatsworth-Tower	Nether End, Baslow	SK 25837214	68

Directions: The car park is at the eastern end of Baslow, marked on maps as Nether End. It is off the A619, by the open space - The Green. A service road loops off the main road to give access to the car park. Pay-and-display. Public toilets.

Starting point locater map for walks 23-30

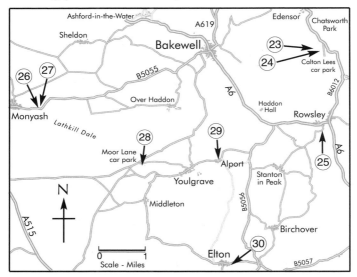

Directions to parking locations and relevant information

Walk	Title (abbreviated)	Starting Point:	Grid reference	Page
23	Chatsworth, Edns.	Calton Lees car park	SK 25906855	70
24	Chatsworth, Swiss.	Calton Lees car park	SK 25906855	72

Directions: From Matlock, or Buxton on the A6. At Rowsley, turn onto the B6012, signed 'Beeley, Baslow, Chatsworth'. In 1 3/4 miles the road crosses the river, go up the hill and take the first turn sharp left, signed 'Calton Lees and Chatsworth Garden Centre'. The car park is on the right. Fee payable at kiosk, except during off-peak times. (A sign states that the car park closes at 7.30pm, it doesn't, that's when the security ends). Provided by the Chatsworth Estate. From Chesterfield on the A619. At the Baslow roundabout, turn left, signed 'Buxton A619, (Rowsley B6012)'. Then keep straight on, ignoring the right turn (A619) to Buxton. Then ignore the next right turn, keeping straight on through Chatsworth Park, passing Edensor village. In just under a mile, the slanting right turn to the car park is immediately after a cattle grid. (2 3/4 miles from the roundabout).

Directions to parking locations and relevant information

Walk	Title	Starting Point:	Grid reference	Page
25	Stanton Moor	Rowsley, lay-by	SK 25686564	74

Directions: From Matlock, or Bakewell on the A6. At Rowsley, turn down School Lane, signed 'Stanton-in-Peak', opposite the Peacock Hotel. Go past the school, and over the bridge. In a few yards the road bends sharp right. Park just after the bend in the lay-by, on the left-hand side adjacent to a play area.

Walk	Title	Starting Point	Grid Reference	Page
26	Bagshaw Dale (abbr.)	Nr. Monyash, lay-by	SK 15756648	76
27	Lathkill Dale (west)	Nr. Monyash, lay-by	SK 15756648	78

Directions: From the A515, Buxton - Ashbourne road. Take the B5055, signed 'Monyash, Bakewell'. Go through the village, in half a mile, on the left hand side is a lay-by. You can also park opposite, near the toilets. From the A6, Matlock to Buxton road: In Bakewell, go up the B5055, not currently signed. It is King Street, running alongside the Rutland Arms Hotel (just before the round-about if coming from Matlock). In 3 1/2 miles the lay-by is on the right.

Walk	Title	Starting Point	Grid Reference	Page
28	Lathkill Dale (central)	Moor Lane car park	SK 19406447	80

Directions: From the A6 Bakewell to Buxton road. In Bakewell town centre, go up the B5055, King Street (see above). In 1/2 mile turn left at the crossroads, signed Youlgrave. In 1 1/2 miles you'll go over Conksbury Bridge. After about a mile, at the top of a hill, the road widens. Turn sharp left and Moor Lane car park is on the right. Pay-and-display. Provided by the National Park Authority. Alternative parking in the wide lay-by at the slanting junction.

Walk	Title	Starting Point	Grid Reference	Page
29	Lathkill Dale (east)	Alport, lay-by	SK 27966456	82

Directions: From the A6, between Bakewell and Rowsley, (1 1/2 miles from Bakewell, 1 mile from Rowsley, take the B5056, signed 'Youlgrave, Ashbourne'. In 1/2 mile ignore the turning left, signed 'Ashbourne B5056'. In 1/2 mile the little village of Alport is reached. There are wide lay-bys to either side.

Walk	Title	Starting Point	Grid Reference	Page
30	Robin Hood's Stride	Elton, roadside	SK 22476094	84

Directions: From the A6, travelling from the north. Go through Bakewell, keep on the A6, and in about 2 1/2 miles, turn right onto the B5056, signed 'Youlgrave, Ashbourne'. In a mile, turn left at the junction, still the B5056 signed 'Ashbourne'. In 2 1/2 miles turn right at a crossroads, signed 'Elton'. On reaching the edge of the village look out for Back Lane on the left. Park after this, just before reaching a little green and a seat on the left, and a bus stop on the right. From the south, on the A6. Turn left at Cromford onto the A5012. Then turn right (still the A5012). In 4 miles, at Grangemill, turn right onto the B5056, signed 'Bakewell'. Ignore the first left turn after 1 1/2 miles. Turn left at a crossroads, after a further 1/2 mile, signed 'Elton'. Then as above.

Walk 1 ~ Bretton Clough & Abney

Start: Lay-by, at the west end of Sir William Hill Road. **GR:** SK22457803.
Map: OS Exp. OL24. **Distance:** 4 ½ miles (7.2km). **Allow:** 2 ½ hours.
Terrain: Sandy track, field paths, moorland paths, stepped sections, short road sections.
Public toilets: None.
Refreshments: None. (However the Barrel Inn, Bretton, is near the start).
Summary of the Walk: A hilly route in this interesting area, rewarding the walker with impressive views over the Dark Peak area. From the higher ground you will see Mam Tor and Kinder Scout to the north-west, and Stanage Edge and the Burbage Rocks area to the north-east. The path above Stoke Ford gives excellent views over Bretton Clough.
Disadvantages: Several steep ascents and descents, some parts, particularly the stepped section into Bretton Clough can be slippery when wet. The path descending from Abney to Stoke Ford can be muddy after rain.
Grading: Difficult. **Ascent:** 850 ft (259m). **Max Height:** 1295ft (395m).

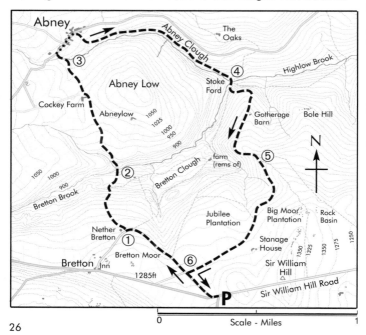

Directions

From the lay-by, walk down the road, in the Bretton direction. In 130 yards turn right onto the wide, walled track. In just over $1/2$ mile the track bends left, passing to the left of a house. Ignore the path sharp right. In 140 yards there is a path signed to the right, at another house.

① Turn right, walking to the right of the house. Bear slightly left down the field towards a wall and a signpost. At the stile go straight on, then go through a gate and slightly right downhill. The path bears right through a gate, down steps, then on the level for 5 yards, before turning left down steps. The path levels out in a 'bowl'. Don't go straight on, turn right along a narrow path, winding down to a footbridge.

② Cross the stream, through a gate, then over a footbridge. The path then ascends and after 320 yards reaches a stile. Go over the stile, follow the path alongside the wall, and through a gap in the wall ahead. Continue straight on, a wall to your right. Go over a stile and in a few yards at the wall corner, go diagonally right to a track and signpost. Turn left, passing to the right of Cockey Farm. At the end of the farm ignore the track which bears left, and walk straight on. Keep the wall to your right for about 80 yards, and at the wall corner turn right, going over a stile. Turn left down the field. The path is indistinct, so walk in the direction of the far left house ahead. Go through the gate at the end of the field.

③ Then go straight on, along a narrow path close to the left-hand side of a stream. In about 60 yards, go through a gate. Follow the path down, cross a footbridge and go up to a gate. Turn right along the road at Abney. In 230 yards, turn right at a signed path, opposite Millhouse Farm. The path descends the valley and in a mile you reach a junction.

④ Turn right, going over two footbridges at Stoke Ford. Then bear right uphill for about 10 yards and turn right at the path junction. In about 20 yards turn left uphill. The route ascends, and bears right to follow a wide grassy path. In $1/3$ mile, go over a stile and in 330 yards is another stile.

⑤ Go over the stile and turn right, alongside the wall. In 50 yards, ignore the path to the left. In $1/4$ mile, turn right over a stile and continue with the wall to your right. In 260 yards go over another stile and straight on, joining a wide track. After $1/2$ mile, go over a stile onto the walled track.

⑥ Turn left and retrace your outward steps back to the road and lay-by.

Walk 2 ~ Eyam Moor

Start: Roadside, Sir William Hill Road. **GR:** SK21027775.
Map: OS Exp. OL24. **Distance:** 4 1/4 miles (6.8 km). **Allow:** 2 1/2 hours.
Terrain: Moorland paths, field paths, farm track and road.
Public toilets: None. **Refreshments:** None.
Summary of the Walk: This excellent walk begins by crossing Eyam Moor, giving great views towards the northern Peak District. It descends into Bretton Clough to the beautifully secluded Stoke Ford. The route then follows an undulating path along a valley, gaining height with expansive views to the north and east. The final part of the walk returns to Eyam Moor, gaining height gradually to the finish. This walk is especially good in July and August, when the heather is in bloom.
Disadvantages: Some sections can be muddy after rain. A short section of road between points 5 and 6, but it is not busy and has good views.
Gradient: Moderate.
Ascent: 700ft (213m). **Max Height:** 1263ft (385ft).

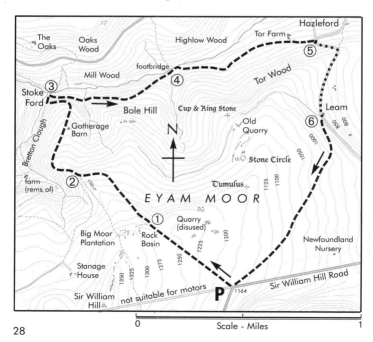

Directions

From the parking area, go over the stile. The cast iron sign reads 'Public Footpath via Stoke Ford to Abney'. The path goes straight ahead, running to the left-hand side of a wall. After half a mile the path forks.

(1) Go straight on (ignore the left-hand path) continuing by the wall. The path descends and bears left away from the wall on the right, to reach a wall straight ahead. A path joins from the left. Turn right to reach a gate and stile. There are lovely views over Bretton Clough and beyond.

(2) Go over the stile and descend the wide grassy path running along the edge of the clough. Go over another stile, the path begins to descend into the clough through hawthorn and oak trees. Ignore the narrow path to the right, go straight on and then turn right at a path junction with a wider path. In a few yards you will see the stream below, crossed by a footbridge. At this point the brook is joined by a stream running in from Abney Clough. The confluence is known as Stoke Ford, but a footbridge has long since replaced the ford. (This is a pleasant spot for a break, with seating across the stream).

(3) Don't descend to the stream (unless having a break of course). Go straight on and follow the path which slants right uphill, away from Stoke Ford. It levels out and descends to cross a stream, before rising again to follow a wire fence. At the path marker post go over the stile and continue by the fence, the path descends by woodland towards a gate.

(4) Cross a stream by a footbridge, ignoring the footbridge to the left, and go over the stile. The path goes up through coniferous trees (this section can be muddy), then over a stile to follow a wall. The wall ends and you cross a field and go through a gate, following a wall to the left. Go through the next gate and straight on, up to another gate. The path widens to become a stony track, as it gains height passing Tor Farm.

(5) Go through gate posts and turn right, walking uphill by a wall to a road. Turn right at the road and follow it uphill. The gradient levels and you pass Leam Farm on the left, 200 yards after this, there is a barn on the left hand side and a footpath signed to the right.

(6) Go over the stile, turn left and follow the path uphill onto Eyam Moor, for the final mile of the walk. The sandy path levels out and follows a wire fence to reach a gate, and the finishing point.

Walk 3 ~ Eyam and Riley Graves

Start: Free car park, or pay-and-display, both on Hawkhill Road, Eyam.
GR: SK21647675 (grid reference given is for free the car park).
Map: OS Exp. OL24. **Distance:** 3 ¾ miles (6 km). **Allow:** 2 hours.
Terrain: Roads in the villages of Eyam and Stoney Middleton. Field paths, stony tracks and woodland paths.
Public toilets: At Hawkhill Road, pay-and-display car park.
Refreshments: Cafés and pub in Eyam. Pub, fish and chip shop, and Indian restaurant in Stoney Middleton.
Summary of the Walk: Eyam is also known as 'The Plague Village', because of the outbreak of the disease in 1665/6. It was caused by a trunk of cloth being sent from London. In the cloth were fleas that carried the plague. The tailor's assistant, George Viccars, was bitten and was the first to die. The villagers lived under a self-imposed isolation to prevent it spreading to other areas. The walk passes all the main points of interest, including the Boundary Stone and Riley Graves.
Disadvantages: Eyam can of course be busy at weekends and Bank Holidays. The lane leading up the hill from Stoney Middleton (between points 5 and 6 on the map) is sometimes used by off-road motorcyclists, usually on Sundays. It is also fairly steep, but pleasantly shaded in hot weather. The route retraces steps for the last ½ mile through Eyam.
Grading: Moderate. **Ascent:** 600ft (182m). **Max Height:** 984ft (300ft).

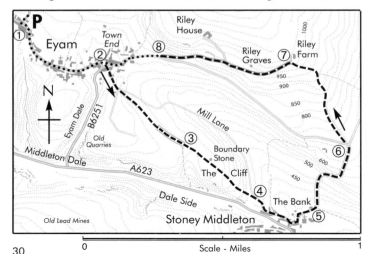

Directions

Leave the car park and turn left, going down Hawkhill Road.

① At the junction, turn left along the main road, Church Street, through Eyam. You will pass Eyam Hall, the 'Information Barn', formerly the Market Hall, three 'plague cottages' and the church. Just after the school the road forks, bear left into an open area - The Square.

② Cross the road and go up Lydgate, a narrow lane with a phone and post box at its junction with The Square. Ignore paths to either side. Pass the 'Unsuitable for motors sign', ignore Mill Lane to the left and go straight on at the footpath signed 'Stoney Middleton, Boundary Stone'.

③ Follow the wide stony track, and go straight on at the footpath sign, on a narrow, walled path. At the end of this, follow the signed path straight on, ignoring the path signed to the right. The prominent rock, with neatly cut holes is the Boundary Stone. (During the plague, villagers left coins in the then vinegar filled holes, in return for supplies. They hoped the vinegar would prevent the disease spreading). Continue past the stone, before descending quite steeply to a gate at a road.

④ Turn right and descend along the road through Stoney Middleton. At a road junction, bear left, continuing downhill. In 100 yards, turn left again at a crossroads. The road passes the church, then bears right past a building known as the 'Roman Baths'. At the bend in the road, ignore the footpath signed straight on at the stile.

⑤ Bear left up the road, past the 'Unsuitable for motors' sign. The road becomes stony, as it climbs quite steeply through woodland.

⑥ At the main road, turn left for a few yards, to avoid crossing at the dangerous blind corner. Cross with great care to the stile and gate, and follow the path uphill alongside a wall. Go through a gate and onto a sandy path through woodland. In a short distance a path joins from the right, continue left going slightly uphill.

⑦ Turn left at the junction with a tarmac lane. After 180 yards on the right is a walled enclosure, inside are Riley Graves. Go over the stile to look at a poignant reminder of the plague. Continue down the lane and at the next junction, turn left (private road to Riley House to right).

⑧ At the junction at the bottom of the hill, turn right to Eyam village centre and retrace your outward steps back to the car park.

Walk 4 ~ Padley Gorge and Longshaw Estate

Start: The side road leading to Grindleford station, off B6251 at Nether Padley (park along the left-hand side of the road). **GR:** SK25107870.
Map: OS Exp. OL24. **Distance:** 4 1/2 miles (7.2 km). **Allow:** 2 1/2 hours.
Terrain: Woodland paths, gravel tracks, field paths, moorland paths.
Public toilets: Adjacent to Longshaw visitors centre.
Refreshments: Station Café, at the start. Café at Longshaw visitors centre. (Fox House Inn and Grouse Inn, both slightly off route, see map).
Summary of the Walk: A varied walk, climbing up through the wooded valley, called Padley Gorge to reach the open country of the National Trust's, Longshaw Estate. A track through the Estate gives great views to the west. After leaving the Estate, the route descends over moorland and through woods to regain the parking area near Grindleford station.
Disadvantages: The route crosses four main roads. Cross with great care.
Grading: Moderate. **Ascent:** 660ft (201m). **Max height:** 1230ft (375m).

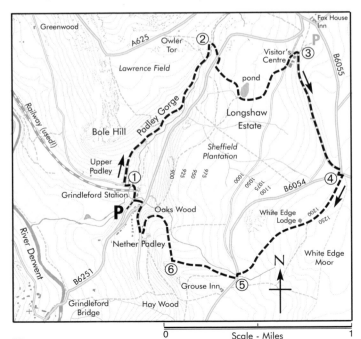

Directions

From the roadside parking, walk past the café and over the railway bridge. Keep on the gravel road, crossing the river. In about 100 yards is a track to the right, signed 'Longshaw Estate, via Padley Gorge'.

① Turn right up the track. In 200 yards go through a gate and follow the slabbed path uphill. At the top of the rise is a building set back to the left. Keep on the main path as it descends and levels out. Ignore the path slanting steeply to the right. The path ascends again and in ¹/₂ mile you leave the woods. Keep straight on, for 200 yards to the footbridge.

② Turn right over the bridge, signed 'Longshaw Visitors Centre'. Walk up to the road. Cross the road and go through a gate, passing a Longshaw Estate information barn. In about 170 yards, ignore a path to the right, keep on the main path going through a gate and in about 250 yards, reaching a pond. Continuing, you pass through three more gates and in ¹/₃ mile you reach a wall ahead with gates to either side. Turn left, passing in front of a millstone. Go through the gate, then take the first path on the right, cross a road and walk to the Visitors Centre. Turn left, when in front of the building. After 30 yards turn right at the junction.

③ Turn right signed 'Wooden Pole car park', pass through a gate and continue on the wide track through the Estate. In just over ¹/₃ mile the track forks. Take the left, higher path and in 280 yards go through a gate to a main road. Turn right along the verge and at the road junction, keep walking right for a few yards. Cross the road via the grassy central reservation. A few yards on the right is a sign for White Edge Moor.

④ Turn right on the wide track and in ¹/₃ mile you pass White Edge Lodge. Continue on the path as it descends moorland to a gate and road. Cross the road and turn left for about 150 yards.

⑤ Turn right at the footpath sign. Bear left, walking with the wall to your left. Ignore the path to the left, signed 'Jubilee'. Continue alongside the wall, going through a gate. In 200 yards, go through a wide gap.

⑥ In a few yards turn diagonally right, following a path across a field. Go through two gates in quick succession, and turn left through woods. In 250 yards the path widens to a track. At the tarmac road turn right, and in 330 yards cross the main road at the junction. Turn right for 40 yards, then left at the signed path, going steeply down to the parking area.

Walk 5 ~ Longshaw Estate

Start: Woodcroft car park, Longshaw Estate. Pay-and-display. Free for National Trust members. **GR:** SK26658006.

Map: OS Exp. OL24. **Distance:** 2½ miles (4.0 km). **Allow:** 1½ hours.

Terrain: Surfaced tracks, grassy paths. Just a few muddy areas. Only one gentle uphill section.

Public toilets: At the Longshaw visitor's centre.

Refreshments: Café at the Longshaw visitor's centre.

Summary of the Walk: A pleasant short walk in the beautiful Longshaw Estate, owned by the National Trust. There are expansive views to the north and west over the Dark Peak hills and valleys. The route follows the main wide track through the estate, before descending to an area of beautiful Scots Pines. A grassy path leads through the estate passing a pond and following a surfaced path back to the visitor's centre and the car park.

Disadvantages: Just one or two potentially muddy areas.

Grading: Easy. **Ascent:** 180ft (55m). **Max. Height:** 1135ft (346m).

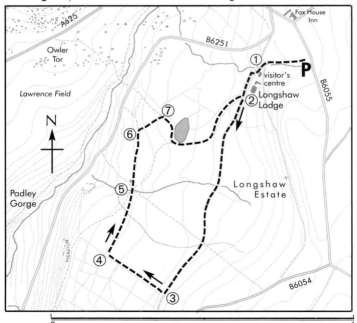

Directions   Walk 5

Follow the wide path down from the car park, signed 'Visitor's Centre'.

① Go over the bridge and turn right, and in about 10 yards turn left, signed 'Visitor's Centre'. When level with the entrance, turn right following the path downhill to the road. At the sign 'Estate walks', cross the road and turn left following a path by a fence for about 80 yards to reach a gate.

② Go through the gate, passing a millstone, ignoring the path to the right and in few yards go through another gate. Continue straight on along the wide track, which gives good views towards the west. Ignore any paths off the main track. After about 3/4 mile the track passes through woodland and ahead is a closed gate.

③ Turn right just before the gate, going through a small gate and follow a path downhill, between a wall on the left and woods to the right. The path ends after about 400 yards at a gate. Go through the gate, into an area of tall Scots Pines. Keep straight on alongside the wall for 40 yards until you reach two gates in the wall. Don't go through the gates.

④ Turn right when level with the first gate, onto a grassy path through the scattered trees.

⑤ After 1/4 mile the path crosses a stream at a path crossroads. Ignore the paths off to the left and right, and keep straight on. The path gains height slightly and in 330 yards there is a path to the right, winding up through trees.

⑥ Turn right onto the path and follow it through the trees. In about 150 yards you will come to a junction with a surfaced track.

⑦ Turn right on the track and in just under 100 yards you reach a lovely pond. Continue past the pond on the wide track. You will pass through three gates, then past a rhododendron grove, to reach the path used at the start of the walk. Turn left past the millstone, and through the gate. Follow the path back to the Visitor's Centre and retrace steps back up to the car park.

Walk 6 ~ Chee Dale

Start: Miller's Dale car park, pay-and-display. **GR:** SK13907330.

Map: OS Exp. OL24. **Distance:** 5 miles (8 km). **Allow:** 3 hours.

Terrain: Field paths. A disused railway line. A steep descent and ascent to cross Flag Dale. The path along Chee Dale is rocky and slippery in places. There are a couple of steep little sections that require care. It can also be very muddy in places, and the stepping stone sections can occasionally be flooded after prolonged rain.

Public toilets: At the car park.

Refreshments: Refreshment van at car park, (weekends - occasional).

Summary of the Walk: From the car park at the disused railway station at Miller's Dale, the route descends steps to the River Wye. Leaving the river it ascends gradually above Chee Dale to the edge of Wormhill. Crossing Flag Dale the walk descends to the River Wye at Chee Dale, a dramatic and craggy dale. The final section follows the Monsal Trail.

Disadvantages: The path along Chee Dale is rocky and slippery in places (see 'Terrain' above for more detail). Descent of 72 steps near the start.

Grading: Difficult. **Ascent:** 630ft (192m). **Max. height:** 1030ft (313m).

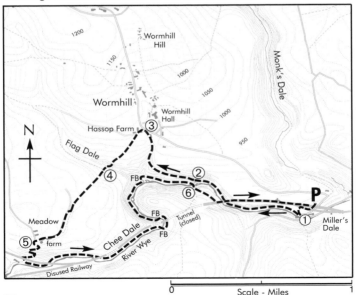

Directions

From the car park, go through the gate to the left of the old station. Turn immediately right, walking along the old platform. At the platform end, bear left and then straight on at a crossroads. The path descends steps.

① At the bottom, turn right through the gap and follow the path by the river. In just under ¹/₂ mile you pass beneath a viaduct. In ¹/₄ mile there is a path to the right, signed 'Wormhill', and a footbridge ahead.

② Turn right, going through the gate at the sign. The path climbs gradually. In ¹/₄ mile the path bends right and dips before ascending to a cottage. 18 yards past the cottage, bear left to a road and a path to the left.

③ Go through the stile, up to the right-hand corner of a corrugated iron barn. Bear left and go through a metal gate, to the right of a stone barn. Go through the gate opposite, at the sign for 'Meadow'. Walk diagonally right to go through a gate. Continue in the same direction to the lower right-hand field corner (out of sight initially). Go through the stile and walk diagonally down the field to a post. Walk to its left and go through a stile. The path descends steeply, in and up out of Flag Dale.

④ Go through the gate, straight on up the field, (parallel with the left-hand wall) then bear right and go through the stile in the wall to your left. Cross the field diagonally right, to the right-hand corner. Go through a gap onto s green lane. Keep straight on between the walls and in 160 yards, turn right through a gate, signed PBW and then left along the road, to reach a farm in 250 yards. Follow the track through the farm.

⑤ About 50 yards after the farm, turn left through a gate, signed 'Chee Dale'. In ¹/₄ mile ignore the path to the right, signed 'PBW'. Keep descending and go through a gate, under a bridge to the river. Turn left, the river to your right. In 180 yards ignore a footbridge and keep to the riverside path. In about ³/₄ mile there are a few stepping stones. In about ¹/₃ mile cross a footbridge, go up steps, ignoring the path to the right. Continue by the river, signed 'Miller's Dale'. Cross another bridge to a longer section of stepping stones. In ¹/₂ mile the path crosses a footbridge, ignore the path left and continue with a stream to your right.

⑥ In ¹/₃ mile turn right, cross a footbridge and bear left for 120 yards. Go straight on at the sign, 'Monsal Trail and Blackwell'. Go through two gates, turn left along the Monsal Trail for ¹/₂ mile to reach the car park.

Walk 7 ~ Monk's Dale

Start: Miller's Dale car park, pay-and-display. **GR:** SK13907330.
Map: OS Exp. OL24. **Distance:** 4 1/2 miles (7.2 km). **Allow:** 2 1/2 hours.
Terrain: Rocky path through Monk's Dale. Field paths, green lanes, river-side path and a disused railway line (Monsal Trail).
Public toilets: At the car park.
Refreshments: Refreshment van at car park, (weekends - occasional).
Summary of the Walk: The upper part of Monk's Dale is as wild and unspoilt a landscape as you will find anywhere in Britain. The dense vegetation vies for space and light, amidst a tangle of moss-covered trees and rocks. The path through the dale is rocky and can be slippery in wet conditions. Leaving the dale the route gains height to pass through Wormhill, and then descends to the eastern end of Chee Dale. The final part follows the Monsal Trail back to the car park.
Disadvantages: The path along Monk's Dale is rocky and often slippery.
Grading: Difficult. **Ascent:** 560ft (171m). **Max. height:** 1090ft (332m).

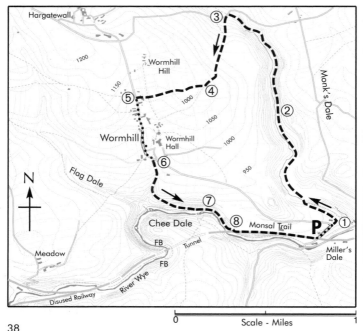

Directions

From the car park return to the road and turn left. In 120 yards, at the corner, turn right through the stile. In 50 yards go through the gate.

① Turn left just before an information board. The path runs to the right of a wall before descending into Monk's Dale. In 250 yards you cross a footbridge and turn left by the side of a stream. The path goes through woods and emerges into an open scrubby area after 1/4 mile. There is a fork in the path, to the left an indistinct path keeps to the stream, whilst a more obvious one climbs slightly. The right-hand path gives the better views, whilst the left-hand one may be wet. They join up in 1/4 mile.

② After a further 320 yards, turn sharp left descending a rocky path into woodland. (You can also go straight on, joining the dale path further on). Go over a stile and straight on. The path along this part of the dale is very rocky and often slippery. In 1/2 mile go over another stile and straight on, leaving the dale and walking over a field towards a road.

③ Go through the stile onto the road and turn left. In about 50 yards, turn left, going through the stile and bear right uphill. In just over 200 yards go through a gate and continue up a walled path. After 1/4 mile nearing the top of the hill, the path bends right and you continue on a walled path. In another 160 yards is a gate.

④ Go through the gate, ignore the stile to the left. Continue along the walled track and in just under 1/2 mile pass a cottage and reach a road.

⑤ Turn left through the strung-out village of Wormhill. In 250 yards the path bears left along a grassy hollow, passing the James Brindley Memorial. Rejoin the road, cross over and in 300 yards, there is a footpath signed to the right, at a slanting junction with a wide track.

⑥ Turn right down the wide track, pass a cottage and go through a gate. Follow the path downhill through woods and in about 200 yards you emerge near the edge of Chee Dale. The path bends left and slants down the valley side, along a limestone pavement. Take care as it can be slippery. In 1/3 mile you reach the bottom of Chee Dale.

⑦ Go through the gate and turn left, following the riverside path. In just under 1/4 mile, a viaduct crosses the river.

⑧ Turn left at the viaduct, climbing steps up to the Monsal Trail. Then turn left, passing an old lime kiln and in 1/2 mile you reach the car park.

Walk 8 ~ Tideswell Dale

Start: Miller's Dale car park, pay-and-display. **GR:** SK13907330.
Map: OS Exp. OL24. **Distance:** 5 ¾ miles (9.2 km). **Allow:** 3 hours.
Terrain: The Monsal Trail (disused railway line), short road sections, field paths, walled tracks, and some stony, occasionally steep paths.
Public toilets: At the car park at the start, also at Tideswell Dale car park.
Refreshments: Refreshment van at car park, (weekends - occasional). Horse and Jockey pub in Tideswell. (Just after point 4, on the map).
Summary of the Walk: The walk starts from the disused Miller's Dale station. It follows the Monsal Trail, before crossing the River Wye and going up the limestone valley of Tideswell Dale. Leaving Tideswell it gains height giving views over the fields and dales of this scenic area, before crossing Monk's Dale and returning to Miller's Dale car park.
Disadvantages: A steep descent which is slippery in wet weather. (after point 7 on the map. The walled tracks can be muddy. Several step-stiles.
Grading: Moderate. **Ascent:** 550ft (168m). **Max. height:** 1050ft (320m).

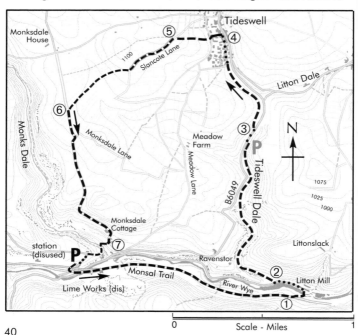

From the car park, go through the gate to the left of the old station building. Go straight on for a few yards and turn left onto a wide path, the Monsal Trail. In just under 1 1/3 miles you pass beneath a bridge. In 35 yards there is a path to the left, signed 'Monsal Trail via Litton Mill'.

① Turn left here and descend a stony path to a footbridge over the River Wye and to the road, at Litton Mill village. Turn left for 300 yards.

② Bear right along a wide path, signed Tideswell Dale. In about 300 yards the path crosses a footbridge to the other side of the stream. In 1/4 mile there is a footbridge to the right. Don't cross it, continue straight on. In 250 yards turn left at a junction, following the path to a car park. At the top right-hand corner take path, signed 'Tideswell village'. Just before reaching a gate, turn left and cross the road. Turn right for 200 yards.

③ Turn left at a public footpath sign. The path gains height, going through a gate, then turns right along a wide track. You shortly pass by some industrial buildings. Ignore the road forking left, go straight on to reach a crossroads. Go straight on into Tideswell. Continue for 300 yards, ignoring side turns. On the left, 20 yards before a pub, is Primrose Lane.

④ Turn left up this narrow lane. At the top, cross the road diagonally right, going through a stile. Follow the path uphill, beside a wall to your right, going over three fields and through three stiles, to reach a walled track.

⑤ Turn left along the track. After 1/3 mile, at a junction of tracks, go straight on through a gate, at a footpath sign. The path is faint. Walk parallel with the wall to the left. At the end of the field, go over a stile at the wall corner and walk alongside the wall, and over a stile to a walled track.

⑥ Turn left and in about 250 yards turn right, going through a gate at a public bridleway sign. The stony track descends to pass Monksdale Cottage, in just over 1/2 mile. Follow the Limestone Way signs, as the track winds down through a gate. In 15 yards there is a path to the right.

⑦ Turn right, following the stony path as it winds steeply downhill into Monk's Dale. At the bottom, cross the stream and walk up to a junction. Turn left, up a narrow stony path. At the top of the rise, bear right at a Nature Reserve board and follow a path up alongside a wall. At the top go straight on through a gate, then through a stile to the road. Turn left down the road for about 120 yards, then turn right into the car park.

Walk 9 ~ Taddington Moor

Start: On Main Street in Taddington, just after the street called Town End (which is on the left) there is a wide grass verge along the right-hand side of the road. (If approaching from Bakewell) **GR:** SK14767103.
Map: OS Exp. OL24. **Distance:** 4 1/4 miles (6.8 km). **Allow:** 2 hours.
Terrain: Walled tracks, field paths, short road sections.
Public toilets: None. **Refreshments:** Pub on Main Street, Taddington.
Summary of the Walk: This short walk gains height from Taddington, giving expansive views over typical White Peak scenery. Returning towards the village, the route passes Sough Top, the highest point of the walk at 1437 feet. (It is also the highest point reached on any of the walks in this book). To the east you will see Monsal Dale and the gritstone edges beyond, and to the north, the moorlands of the Dark Peak. Taddington may hold the record for England's earliest bypass, completed in 1938.
Disadvantages: Numerous step-stiles towards the end of the walk. Two short road sections. Some sections can be muddy.
Grading: Moderate.
Ascent: 570ft (174m). **Maximum height:** 1437ft (438m).

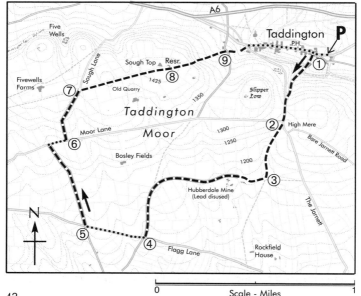

Directions

From the suggested parking area, walk up the road towards the village. In about 100 yards on the left, you pass the Bramwell Memorial Institute building. Immediately after this is a lane, signed Dokindale Road.

① Turn left going up the stony, walled track, as it gradually ascends away from the village. Ignore paths to the left and right, keeping straight on as you gain height, reaching a road junction after about 1/3 mile.
Turn left along the road and in 200 yards there is a road to the right. At the junction corner, a footpath is signed to the right.

② Go over the stile at the sign and descend the field diagonally right to a gap in the wall at the field corner. Continue straight on, down the next field. Go over a stile at the wall and continue straight on. Before reaching the stile in the wall ahead, look to the right - you will see a gate.

③ Turn right and go through the gate. Follow the right-hand wall through a field of grassy humps and hollows, the remnants of lead mining. At the end of the field, go through the gate onto a walled track. (This can be muddy in winter). Follow the stony track for 3/4 mile as it descends gradually to a road junction.

④ Turn right along the road. It isn't busy but take great care.

⑤ In 1/3 mile, turn right at a crossroads, up a lane signed 'Limestone Way'. In about 1/2 mile, turn right at the road junction, again signed 'Limestone Way'. In 150 yards, there is a track to the left.

⑥ Turn left up the track, signed 'Limestone Way'. In 1/3 mile a gate crosses the track, with paths to either side just before the gate.

⑦ Turn right, at the signed footpath, going over the stile and following the path alongside the left-hand wall. The path crosses seven small fields, with seven stiles, before you reach the right-hand side of a covered reservoir at Sough Top.

⑧ From the reservoir, walk diagonally right across the field to a signpost. Go over the stile and walk diagonally right downhill. Go through a stile at a broken wall and continue diagonally right downhill, to a road.

⑨ Cross the road and go through two stiles in quick succession. Go straight on down the field. Go over a stile and descend a narrow path to reach a road at Taddington. Turn left for a few yards, then right at the junction. Walk down the road through the village, back to the car.

Walk 10 ~ Cressbrook Dale and Miller's Dale

Start: Roadside parking, adjacent to Cressbrook Mill. **GR:** SK17377275.
Map: OS Exp. OL24. **Distance:** 5 1/2 miles (9km). **Allow:** 3 hours.
Terrain: Quiet lanes. Paths along dales, which can be muddy. Field paths.
Public toilets: None. (The nearest are at Monsal Head).
Refreshments: D's Brew Stop, near Cressbrook Mill (weekends only).
Summary of the Walk: The walk follows a lane into Cressbrook Dale. It
gains height to give great views over the dale and surrounding landscape.
Another lane is followed before descending into Miller's Dale, and walk-
ing past the former Litton Mill (now residential). The final section follows
the River Wye, along the attractive Miller's Dale to finish at the road near
Cressbrook Mill (also now residential).

Disadvantages: Some road walking (but quiet lanes). Three moderate
ascents. The path along Miller's Dale can occasionally flood (there is an
indicated alternative route, if this is the case).

Grading: Moderate. **Ascent:** 770ft (234m). **Max. height:** 1050ft (320m).

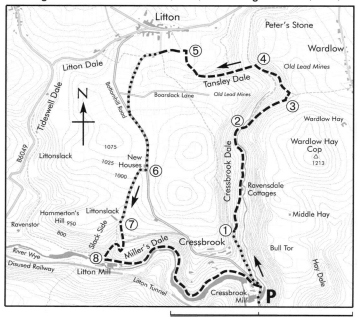

Directions

From the lay-by, walk straight on uphill on a road signed, 'Cressbrook and Litton'. (Ignore the road to the left).

① After nearly ½ mile, turn right, signed 'Ravensdale - No Through Road', following the narrow lane downhill. In ⅓ mile you descend into Cressbrook Dale and pass to the left of Ravensdale Cottages. Keep straight on at a footpath sign, going through a gate into woodland. In just under ¼ mile the path narrows and passes over a footbridge. In 150 yards there is a fork in the path.

② Bear right taking the uphill path (you can avoid the hill by continuing straight on along the dale bottom, see map). The path climbs for ⅓ mile and reaches the dale edge at a wall corner.

③ Bear left just after the wall corner following a path downhill, back into the dale. At the bottom bear right and walk with the wall to your left. In 160 yards there are stepping stones across what is often a dry stream.

④ Turn left going over the stepping stones, go through a gate and walk up the dale (Tansley Dale). Towards the top of the dale, after ⅓ mile, the path turns right and goes up alongside a wall to a stile at a wall corner. Go over the stile and bear right up to a wall corner and signpost. Then bear right again, walking to a gate and signpost.

⑤ Go over the stile, to the side of the gate and turn left on the walled track. In 250 yards turn left and follow the road. In ½ mile you pass a cemetery and in a further ⅓ mile you pass a row of houses.

⑥ Just after the last house turn right onto a lane, signed 'Littonslack'. In just over ⅓ mile the road ends at the hamlet of Littonslack.

⑦ Go over the stile and walk straight on along a grassy path. In 250 yards ignore the path signed to the left and continue on the wide track as it bends down into the dale. Turn left at the bottom, walking along the dale and then go over a stile and straight on down a lane.

⑧ Turn left at the road and go between the gate posts at the entrance to the former Litton Mill, signed 'concession path'. At the end of the buildings the path bends right and then left, going through a gate into Miller's Dale. Follow the riverside path and in 1¼ miles go over a footbridge. Bear left, ignoring the path to the right, walking with a wall to your right. Go past Cressbrook Mill to the road and the finish.

Walk 11 ~ Monsal Head and Miller's Dale

Start: Long stay car park, behind Monsal Head. **GR:** SK18527148.
Map: OS Exp. OL24.
Distance: 6 miles (9.6km).
Allow: 3 hours.
Terrain: Disused railway lines. Farm tracks, paths across fields.
Public toilets: At the car park.
Refreshments: Café and pub at Monsal Head.
Summary of the Walk: Starting from Monsal Head, one of the most scenic spots in the Peak District, the walk descends to the Monsal Trail at a viaduct. It then leaves the Trail, gaining height to give great views down into Monsal Dale and across the surrounding hills. It then passes through the hamlet of Brushfield and goes up fields to another panoramic viewpoint overlooking Miller's Dale, 600 feet below. The views continue as the route descends to the dale, to rejoin the Monsal Trail. The final section follows the River Wye, before finishing up back on the disused railway line with a short climb back up to Monsal Head.

Disadvantages: A short steep descent into and out of Monsal Dale. The section along the River Wye, between the former Litton and Cressbrook Mills, can occasionally flood. If you don't want to get your feet wet there is a signed alternative route, but it's more fun to paddle.

Grading: Moderate.
Ascent: 630ft (192m).
Maximum height: 1099ft (335m).

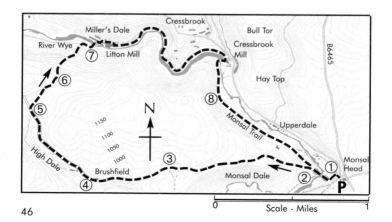

Directions

From the car park, walk to the right of the Monsal Head Hotel and turn left on the road to the corner. Go through the wide gap in the wall and turn right, signed 'Upperdale and Monsal Viaduct'. Walk down the steps and in 60 yards is a bench and a sign 'Viaduct and Monsal Trail'.

① Turn left descending steeply to the Monsal Trail. Turn right, going over the viaduct. 65 yards after the viaduct turn left at a sign for 'Brushfield'.

② Go through the gate and continue straight on, walking uphill (ignore path to left). The stony path winds uphill. In $^1/_3$ mile the path joins a wider track. Bear left, continuing uphill. In $^3/_4$ mile at the third gate, the track ends. Continue straight on, with a wall to your left. At the end of the field is a wide gap, with a tree to your left and a sign, 'Brushfield'.

③ Go straight on following the sign, along a wide track. In $^1/_2$ mile, after a third gate you pass by some holiday homes (a former farm).

④ Turn right at the road junction, going uphill, signed 'Priestcliffe and Miller's Dale'. The wide track winds uphill passing to the right of a working farm. In just over $^1/_2$ mile is a stile and footpath signed to the right.

⑤ Turn right, going over the stile and walk uphill, with a wall to your right. In 280 yards, at the top of the field, is a stile in the wall ahead.
Go over the stile and turn right, walking alongside an old lead rake. In 130 yards, the obvious path goes downhill to a stile at a fence corner.

⑥ Go over the stile and turn left downhill, going over another stile in 210 yards. Continue descending steeply for $^1/_3$ mile, before going over a stile and turning right down steps to the disused railway. Turn right for 30 yards to a seat and sign 'Monsal Trail link via Litton Mill'.

⑦ Turn left at the sign, descending steps, then crossing a footbridge to a road. Turn right, signed 'Cressbrook'. In about 150 yards go between the gate posts at the entrance to the former Litton Mill, signed 'concession path'. Follow the wide road past the buildings and on into Miller's Dale. Follow the riverside path and in $1^1/_4$ miles go over a footbridge. Then go straight on, ignore a path to the left. In 30 yards go over another footbridge and up steps. At the top go straight on, on a path signed 'Monsal Trail'. In $^1/_3$ mile you pass through a gate.

⑧ Turn left on the Monsal Trail and in just under a mile go over the viaduct. At the end of the viaduct turn left uphill and retrace your outward steps.

Walk 12 ~ Magpie Mine and Deep Dale

Start: Car park, off Fennel Street, Ashford-in-the-Water. Free.
GR: SK19486975. Or park at the lay-by near Sheepwash Bridge.
Map: OS Exp. OL24. **Distance:** 6 ½ miles (10.4km). **Allow:** 3 hours.
Terrain: Paths over fields, through woodland and alongside the River Wye. Three short road sections.
Public toilets: At the car park.
Refreshments: Two pubs in Ashford-in-the-Water. Pub in Sheldon.
Summary of the Walk: A walk full of interest, starting from the beautiful village of Ashford-in-the-Water. Climbing from the village there are great views over the valley, before the ruins of Magpie Mine come into sight. The distinctive building used to house a Cornish beam engine, installed in 1840 to pump water from the 700 foot deep level. In 1833 there was a dispute between rival miners resulting in three deaths, caused by fires being lit underground. Leaving Sheldon the walk descends to Deep Dale, which has a variety of plantlife. It then goes through woodland, before descending to the River Wye. The final part follows the meandering river and crosses the main road, back to Ashford.
Disadvantages: A couple of fairly steep ascents. Two short road sections. Some parts can be muddy in winter. Several step-stiles.
Grading: Moderate. **Ascent:** 750ft (229m). **Max. height:** 1082ft (330m).

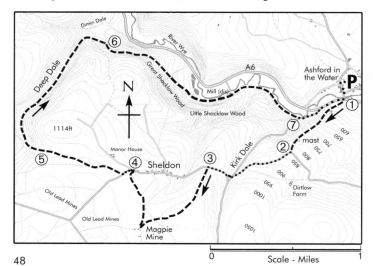

From the car park, walk back to the road junction. Turn left along Fennel Street. Where the road bends sharp left, continue straight on crossing the bridge (Sheepwash Bridge). Then cross the main road (take care).

① At the footpath sign, go through a gate and follow a tarmac track uphill. After passing a house the route is on grass as it continues to climb, passing in front of a mast. The path bears slightly left to a gate and a road.

② Turn right along the road, in just under $^1/_2$ mile you come to a junction. Cross the road and go over the stile opposite and up the field to a gate. Turn right on the road for about 230 yards, to a track on the left.

③ Turn left along the signed walled track as it ascends gradually to open fields. In $^1/_3$ mile go over a stile and continue straight on towards the chimney at Magpie Mine. After 250 yards go straight on at a footpath crossroads. In a few yards go over a stile and then bear left to the mine. With your back to the largest building and the round chimney to your right, bear slightly left and follow a path to the right of a wall. Go over a stile and straight on over a field to a stile. Go straight on to a gate into an enclosure. Ignore the gate in the wall slightly right. Go straight on and through a gate, signed public footpath. The path keeps to the left of a wall, to a stile. A signed path then goes diagonally over the field to a stile at the top right-hand corner. Continue straight on, with buildings to your right, to a gate onto the road.

④ Turn left along the road for 120 yards, then turn right at the stile and a footpath sign. Go straight on over the field to a stile. Turn left and in a few yards go over a stile. Bear right to the wall corner, ignore the stile to the left. Go through a gate, continue by the right-hand wall for $^1/_3$ mile.

⑤ Go over a stile and descend into Deep Dale. Go over a stile at the bottom, and turn right. In a few yards turn right through a gate and then left down the dale. In just over $^1/_2$ mile the path contours right to a sign.

⑥ Keep straight on signed 'Ashford, Sheldon'. The path undulates through woodland. Ignore any side paths, keep to the well-defined main route. The path descends to the River Wye and passes a disused mill. The riverside path reaches a road after about $^1/_2$ mile.

⑦ Turn left and at the main road, turn right. In about 250 yards cross the road, with care, to go over Sheepwash Bridge and back to the car park.

Walk 13 ~ Monsal Dale and the River Wye

Start: Car park, off Fennel Street, Ashford-in-the-Water. Free.
GR: SK19486975. Or park at the lay-by, near Sheepwash Bridge.
Map: OS Exp. OL24. **Distance:** 6 miles (9.6 km). **Allow:** 3 hours.
Terrain: Field paths, walled lanes, path through Monsal Dale, woodland path and a short road section.
Public toilets: At the car park at the start and at Monsal Head.
Refreshments: Pubs in Ashford. Pub and café at Monsal Head.
Summary of the Walk: A lovely walk starting from the attractive village of Ashford-in-the-Water. It gains height gradually to reach Monsal Head, a viewpoint over the beautiful Monsal Dale. From there the route descends steeply to a weir on the River Wye. The meandering river is followed through Monsal Dale, until the path crosses the A6 road. It gains height to pass through the attractive Great Shacklow Wood before descending back to join the river, and on to Ashford-in-the-Water.
Disadvantages: A steep descent and a fairly steep ascent. A short road section. Some parts can be muddy in winter.
Grading: Moderate. **Ascent:** 650ft (198m). **Max. height:** 880ft (268m).

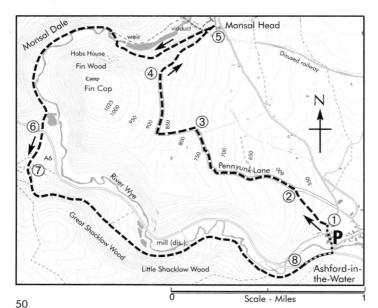

Directions   Walk 13

From the car park, walk back to the road junction. Turn right up
Vicarage Lane. Cross the road and continue for about 70 yards.

① Turn sharp left up the path signed 'Monsal Dale'. It goes up by the side
of a fence to a stile. Go through the stile and bear slightly to the right
across the field, passing a guide post, and on to a stile at a wall.

② Go over the stile and turn left along a walled track, Pennyunk Lane.
Continue along the lane to its end, in just under ³/4 mile.

③ Turn left, going through the stile, walking up the field, alongside a wall.
At the top go through a gate and turn right, signed 'Monsal Dale'. Pass
a dew pond and go through a gate onto a walled track. Go through two
more gates and proceed to the third and final gate.

④ Go through the gate and bear right at sign for 'Monsal Head', passing
two seats. Continue along the path as it keeps to the edge of the dale.
In ¹/3 mile the path descends, to reach a slanting path junction.

⑤ Turn sharp left, descending into the dale. (If you wish to visit Monsal
Head for the view and facilities, turn right here, going uphill for 20 yards
and through a stile). At the weir, turn left and in 100 yards cross a footbridge and turn left. A broad path follows Monsal Dale, there are several narrower paths leaving the main path, looping left to the riverside,
which can be followed if you wish. In just under a mile you'll come to a
sign 'White Lodge and A6'. Continue straight on, ignoring the path to
the right, going over a stream and up to the road at a gap stile.

⑥ Cross the road with great care, go up the steps, then turn left for a few
yards and then right. Go through a gate and straight on. In about 100
yards, ignore the path to the right, signed 'Taddington'. Go straight on,
the path becoming rockier as it climbs alongside a stream, with a wall
to the left. Turn left, going over a stile at the sign 'Ashford, Deep Dale,
Sheldon'. The rocky path winds upwards to reach a path junction.

⑦ Turn left at the sign 'Ashford, Sheldon'. The path undulates through
woodland. Ignore any side paths, keep to the well-defined main route.
After about ³/4 mile the path descends to the River Wye and passes a
disused mill. The riverside path reaches a road after about ¹/2 mile.

⑧ Turn left and at the main road, turn right. In about 250 yards cross the
road, to go over Sheepwash Bridge and walk straight on to the car park.

Walk 14 ~ Great Longstone and the Monsal Trail

Start: Great Longstone, roadside parking on the opposite side of the road to the Crispin Inn. **GR:** SK19807190. Please don't obstruct any gateways.
Map: OS Exp. OL24. **Distance:** 4 miles (6.4 km). **Allow:** 2 hours.
Terrain: Green lanes, field paths, short road sections, Monsal Trail.
Public toilets: None.
Refreshments: The Crispin Inn and The Red Lion in Great Longstone.
Summary of the Walk: From the attractive village of Great Longstone the walk follows a green lane meandering above the village, giving views towards Monsal Dale and beyond. The route descends through the small village of Rowland, and joins the Monsal Trail for a short distance, before crossing fields back into Great Longstone.
Disadvantages: The Monsal Trail is very popular with cyclists, especially at weekends. It is plenty wide enough to accommodate everyone, but it does mean that you have to be aware of bikes. Several step-stiles and two short road sections.
Grading: Easy. **Ascent:** 260ft (79m). **Maximum height:** 820ft (250m).

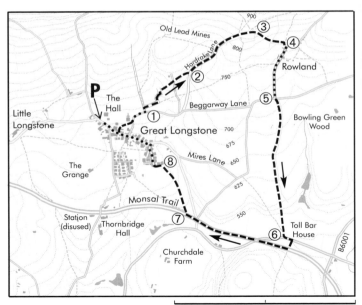

Walk along the road, the green to the right. In about 150 yards turn left up a road, signed 'Footpath To Church'. In a few yards, turn right at a gate, then through another gate. Take the path passing by the church, to a road. Go through the stile and turn left along the road.

① In 150 yards turn left at a footpath sign onto a green lane. In a few yards on the right, go through a stile and cut the field corner to another stile. Turn right and in 100 yards follow the lane round the bend (ignore stile ahead). In 150 yards the lane ends. Go through the stile on the right, uphill with a wall to the right. At the top, bear left to the step-stile, to the left of a gate. Cross a track, and go through a stile. The path bears left, to a gap in a wall. Descend the field corner to a stile.

② Turn left, onto a green lane. In 330 yards, the walls of the lane diverge. Keep to the right-hand wall. In 180 yards go through a stile and straight on, in a few yards to a stile. Walk with a wall to your left. In 70 yards at the wall corner, bear slightly right, walking in a line towards a buff coloured dome ahead. In 160 yards there is a stile near a wall corner.

③ Go over the stile and straight on towards a tree at a wall corner. Go through a stile and walk with a wall to your right. Go over the stile at the wall corner, turn left and in a few yards go through a stile to a road.

④ Turn right along the road for 1/3 mile, through the hamlet of Rowland.

⑤ At the junction, cross the road diagonally left to a wall corner. Follow the path leaving the road, alongside the wall. The path runs for 1/2 mile alongside the wall, going over three step-stiles. 100 yards after the final stile, the path leaves the wall. You bear slightly right down a field towards a gate, to the right of a house. Go over the stile to the road.

⑥ Cross the road, turn left for 80 yards and then right at the gate, opposite Toll Bar House. Go across the field, through the gate to the Monsal Trail. Turn right and in just over 1/2 mile, you go over a second road.

⑦ After 100 yards, turn right at the sign, 'Great Longstone'. Go down a few steps, and in 20 yards, turn left through a stile. Take the distinct path straight ahead (ignore the fainter path to the left). The path goes through two stiles and after 1/3 mile reaches a gate.

⑧ Go through the gate and turn left. In 30 yards turn right along a road. In 180 yards is a junction. Turn right and at the main road, turn left through the village. Pass the The Crispin Inn, to return to the start point.

Walk 15 ~ Bakewell and the Monsal Trail

Start: Bakewell Bridge, pay-and-display car park. Off Coombs Road.
GR: SK22056865.
Map: OS Exp. OL24. **Distance:** 3 1/4 miles (5.2 km). **Allow:** 1 1/2 hours.
Terrain: Footpaths, green lane (can be muddy), disused railway track.
Public toilets: Bakewell town centre.
Refreshments: Choice of cafés and pubs in Bakewell. Café en route at
The Country Bookshop, (at the old Hassop station).
Summary of the Walk: This short walk leaves Bakewell by the River
Wye. It soon gains height, giving panoramic views, before descending to
the Monsal Trail and returning to Bakewell.
Disadvantages: Parts of the walk can be muddy, and there is one fairly
steep section, (between Points 2 and 3). You need to be aware of cyclists
on the Monsal Trail.
Grading: Easy. **Ascent:** 375ft (114m). **Max. height:** 689ft (210m).

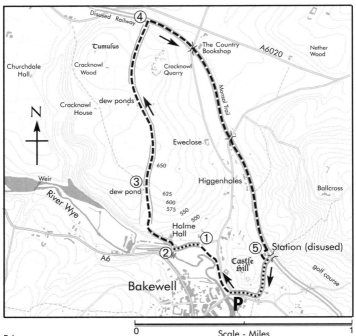

Leave the car park by the gap at the corner (near the river and the road bridge). Cross the road (take care) and go through a gate opposite, signed Scott's Garden, walking initially by the river. After going through a gate the river bends left. Bear slightly left, crossing a field to a gate.

① Turn left along the lane for about 200 yards.

② Turn right up a lane, signed as a Bridleway (opposite a slabbed bridge, Sheepwash Bridge). In 90 yards bear left still going uphill. The lane becomes stony and rises fairly steeply passing to the left of some old mine buildings. You then pass through a gate to a field. Follow the track up the field. In 230 yards you leave the track at a marker post and continue straight on over grass. In 130 yards you pass to the right of a dew pond with a gate ahead.

③ Go through the gate and along the walled track. There is another gate in 200 yards. In 150 yards the track reaches its highest point, with good views ahead. The track descends gently for just over $1/2$ mile, before a short steeper downhill section brings you to a gate and the Monsal Trail.

④ Turn right along the wide track. In $1/4$ mile the track goes under a bridge. (In 80 yards is a gate to the left, giving access to The Country Bookstore). In 200 yards on the left is a grassy picnic area. Continuing on, you pass beneath another bridge in just under $1/3$ mile. In a further $1/2$ mile there is an elegant stone building to the right and a bridge ahead. This is the former Bakewell station.

⑤ Turn right off the trail, at the nearest corner of the old station. Cross the car park to the exit, and turn left along the road (Station Road). In 35 yards ignore the road joining from the left and continue on Station Road as it bends right and descends towards the town. (The view over Bakewell is dominated by the Cattle Market. There are rumours that some people like it). In $1/3$ mile you reach a slanting junction with Coombs Road. Cross the road and go through a gap in the wall, back into the car park and the finish.

Walk 16 ~ Bakewell and Haddon Hall

Start: Bakewell Bridge, pay-and-display car park. **GR:** SK22056865.
Map: OS Exp. OL24. **Distance:** 5 ¾ miles (9.2 km) **Allow:** 3 hours.
Terrain: Footpaths, tracks, two roadside sections and a riverside path.
Public toilets: The town centre, the Park and near the Cattle Market.
Refreshments: Cafés and pubs in Bakewell.
Summary of the Walk: From Bakewell the route soon gains height, with one fairly steep section. The walk then crosses pastures to reach a lane before again crossing the pastures of Haddon Fields. It descends to give a great view of Haddon Hall. The final section follows the River Wye.
Disadvantages: The final riverside section can be very muddy after rain. There are two short sections along roads. There is a busy road to cross (with a pedestrian reservation) the A6, at Haddon Hall.
Grading: Moderate. **Ascent:** 440ft (134m). **Max. height:** 682ft (208m).

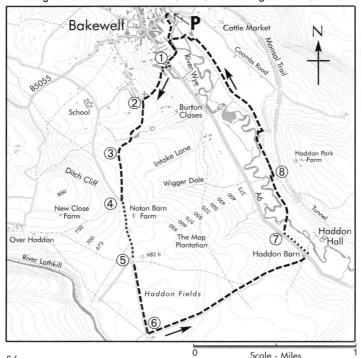

Leave the car park by the gap at the corner (near the river/road bridge). Turn left over the bridge. After the bridge, turn left and follow the path by the river, going past two footbridges. In about 90 yards the the river bends left. Continue straight on into a park. The path bears right to a toilet block. Take the narrow path straight on to the main road.

① Cross the road by the pedestrian crossing, turn left. After 23 yards turn right on a road. In 53 yards turn right up Park Road and cross to the left pavement. In 50 yards is Park View. Cross over and go through the gate. Keep straight on, go up the steps, and reach a T junction in $1/4$ mile.

② Turn left, signed 'footpath'. In 90 yards are two stiles in succession. Walk straight on with a wall to your left for 130 yards. Then go through a gate onto a walled path. In 130 yards the right-hand wall ends. Bear left for 80 yards to a little waterlogged area. Then turn right walking up the slope and in 130 yards go through a gap and bear left (arrowed) uphill. At the top of the rough steps, bear right over a field to a gate.

③ Turn left going gently uphill and in 320 yards, go through the gate at the far corner. Continue straight on, uphill to a gate at the far corner.

④ Turn left along the road for just over $1/3$ rd mile to a sharp right bend.

⑤ Go straight on, signed 'Restricted Byway'. In $1/4$ mile go through a gate and in another $1/4$ mile is a path crossroads. Ignore a gate to the right.

⑥ Turn left just before buildings and walk with the wall to your right. In $1/3$ mile go through a gate. In 350 yards go through a gate and continue downhill. In 140 yards go straight on, at a crossroads. In $1/4$ mile, go through a gate descending a track to the road. Cross over and turn left.

⑦ In 370 yards turn right at a stile (easily missed). In 200 yards descend to a footbridge. In $1/3$ rd mile, turn right on a road. Walk for 25 yards.

⑧ Turn left, signed Bridleway. In 350 yards keep straight on (bridleway to the right). In 50 yards take the lower path, bearing left down steps to the river. Don't go over the footbridge, turn right and go over a stile. Turn left, signed 'Bakewell'. In 320 yards bear left, over two footbridges, then go diagonally left. Go through the gate at the footpath sign, the hedge to your left. In $1/3$ mile, after three more gates, turn left. Cross the road, turn right. Follow the tarmac path and in 150 yards pass by toilets. Go straight on, over a footbridge. Turn right, retracing steps to the finish.

Walk 17 ~ Baslow Edge

Start: Roadside, Calver Bridge, school lay-by or Dukes Road.
GR: SK24737435 (grid reference given is for the school lay-by only).
Map: OS Exp. OL24. **Distance:** 4 ¾ miles (7.6 km). **Allow:** 3 hours.
Terrain: Paths across fields, minor roads, stony tracks.
Public toilets: None, but toilets, off-route at Nether End, Baslow.
Refreshments: Pub near the start. Café at Derbyshire Craft Centre, near the start. Pubs in Nether End, Baslow (slightly off-route).
Summary of the Walk: This varied walk leaves Calver Bridge, following the River Derwent. A minor road then leads to Bubnell and Baslow, the route then climbs steadily up to Baslow Edge. There are great views from Baslow Edge over Chatsworth Estate to the south and the hills and valleys to the east and north.
Disadvantages: About 1 ¼ miles of walking on minor roads (pavements most of the way). A steady ascent to reach Baslow Edge.
Grading: Moderate. **Ascent:** 750ft (229m). **Max. height:** 984ft (300m).

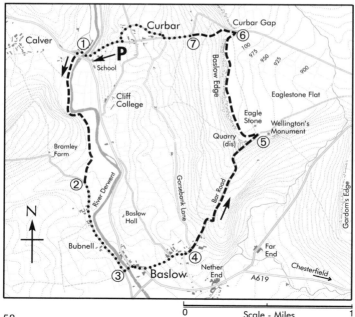

Directions

Walk by the Bridge Inn. Go over the footbridge, next to the road bridge.

① Cross the road and take the path signed 'Subway' and 'Public Footpath'. In 180 yards, go through a gate and follow the path by the river. At the end of the field, go through a stile and turn left. Follow the path as it bends right, with a wall to the left. In $1/4$ mile the path veers to the right away from the wall and you go through a stile, crossing a field to a gate.

② Go through the gate and turn left on the road. It shortly runs by the river and in $1/2$ mile you pass a weir. In 150 yards is a road to the left.

③ Turn left here, crossing the River Derwent by an arched bridge. Bear right on the pavement for a few yards and cross the road at the pedestrian reservation. Turn right for 100 yards and bear left at the mini-roundabout, up School Lane. Ignore roads off and in just over $1/4$ mile you reach a triangular green. Bear left up Bar Road. Keep straight on, ignoring side roads and in 330 yards you reach the end of the tarmac.

④ Go straight on, passing the 'Restricted Byway' sign. Ignore any side paths, as the gravelly track steadily climbs. In $1/2$ mile you go through a gate and in 250 yards reach the end of the ascent. (The stone cross of Wellington's Monument is a 150 yard optional diversion straight on).

⑤ Turn acute left on a narrow path leading along Baslow Edge. (not left along the broad track, which goes past a prominent rock, signed with a blue arrow). Our path more or less keeps to the edge. In $3/4$ mile you pass a view indicator. Continue on to reach a path junction.

⑥ At the junction with a wider path, turn left and then go through the left of two gates. Don't go to the road, but turn left on a narrow path running alongside and above the road. (It may be overgrown in summer). In 180 yards turn left through a gate at a footpath and National Trust sign. Follow the path downhill, go through a stile, keeping a wall to your right. Then go through another stile, going straight on to a gate. Descend the field with a wall to your left, to a stile and onto the road.

⑦ Turn left down the road, after 250 yards, turn left along a road called The Green. Then ignore the two roads leaving to the left. At the junction go straight on, down Pinfold Hill. At the next junction turn right, going down the hill (take care, as it can be busy) for $1/4$ mile to the junction at the Bridge Inn and to your chosen parking area.

Walk 18 ~ Froggatt Edge

Start: Roadside at Calver Bridge, school lay-by, or on Dukes Road.
GR: SK24737435 (grid reference given for the school lay-by only).
Map: OS Exp. OL24. **Distance:** 6 ¾ miles (10.8 km). **Allow:** 4 hours.
Terrain: Riverside paths, woodland and sandy paths along the edges.
Public toilets: None. (The nearest ones are at Nether End, Baslow).
Refreshments: The Bridge Inn and the café at the Derbyshire Craft Centre, both near the the parking areas.
Summary of the Walk: From Calver Bridge the route follows the River Derwent before climbing up steeply through woodland to Froggatt Edge and then along Curbar Edge. There are expansive views along the Edges. The final part descends to Curbar village and down the road to the finish.
Disadvantages: The section between points 4 and 5, is quite steep as it climbs up through Hay Wood. The final part of the walk is on tarmac, although the walk through Curbar village is pleasant enough.
Grading: Moderate. **Ascent:** 770ft (235m). **Max. height:** 1099ft (335m).

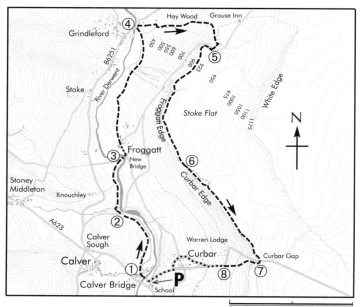

Directions

Walk past the Bridge Inn. Cross the river by the pedestrian bridge.

① Turn right in 25 yards, opposite the sign for 'Calver Mill'. The road crosses a campsite to a gate. The path crosses a field to a riverside path.

② In just over ¼ mile you reach a road. Cross over and go through a stile. In 150 yards, turn right over a footbridge and continue by the river.

③ In ½ mile is a road. Turn right, over the bridge. Turn left at the junction, along Hollowgate. Use the raised footway on the right, then cross the road and go along Spooner Lane, signed 'Grindleford Bridge'. At the end of lane, go through a stile, a marker post signs diagonally right across a field to a stile. Turn left and at the broken wall keep straight on at a stile, and a sign for Froggatt Wood. After crossing a stream, ignore a path signed to the right. At the end of the woods, in just under ¼ mile, go through the gate and descend by a wall and across a stream. The path goes diagonally right over a field to a stile and onto the road.

④ Turn right along the road. In 40 yards turn right at a footpath sign. Follow the unmade road to its end. Turn left, signed Froggatt Edge. In 300 yards at a wall corner, ignore the path signed left, and bear right still uphill. In 380 yards at a fork, keep right reaching a gate in 180 yards. Keep straight on for 200 yards, then bear right at a junction. After 50 yards the path descends to cross a stream and climbs to a road.

⑤ Cross the road, and turn right. Go through the gate on the left onto a wide path. In ½ mile go through a gate. In a further ½ mile ignore a path signed sharp right. In 380 yards is a post marked with an arrow.

⑥ Go straight on, keeping to the edge as the main path veers left. (You can just stay on the wide path if you wish). In 350 yards bear right at a junction to rejoin the wide path in 105 yards. Turn right and in ¾ mile go through a gate and in 10 yards turn right, going downhill to cross a road.

⑦ Just before the gate ahead, turn right on a path above the road. In 180 yards turn left at a gate. Follow the path downhill, go through a stile keeping a wall to your right. Then through a stile, ignore the path to the left. Go through a gate, descending the field to a stile onto the road.

⑧ Turn left, and in 250 yards turn right along The Green. Ignore the two roads to the left and in ¼ mile go straight on at a crossroads. At the next junction turn right, and descend for ¼ mile to the parking area.

Walk 19 ~ Bramley Wood and Calver

Start: Calver Bridge, roadside. Service road near school and Dukes Road.
GR: SK24737435 (grid reference given for the school lay-by only).
Map: OS Exp. OL24. **Distance:** 4¾ miles (7.6 km). **Allow:** 3 hours.
Terrain: Paths across pasture, minor roads and woodland paths.
Public toilets: None.
Refreshments: Café at Derbyshire Craft Centre, near start. Pubs in Calver.
Summary of the Walk: This walk leaves Calver Bridge, following the
River Derwent, then gains height with views across to the gritstone edges.
It then follows paths above woodland, before descending back to Calver.
In May there are bluebells and rhododendrons in the woods.
Disadvantages: There are three sections along minor roads. A steep
descent at the end of Bramley Wood to Calver, which can be slippery after
rain (between points 8 and 9). There are several step-stiles.
Grading: Moderate. **Ascent:** 460ft (140m). **Max. height:** 787ft (240m).

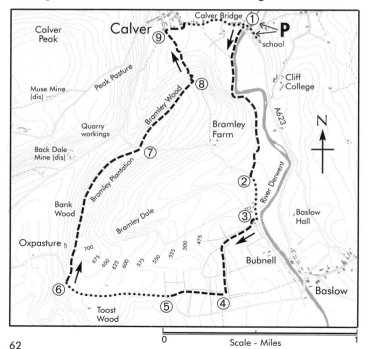

Directions

Walk by the Bridge Inn. Go over the footbridge, next to the road bridge.

① Cross the road and take the path signed 'Subway'. In 180 yards, go through a gate and follow the path by the river. At the end of the field, go through a stile and turn left. Follow the path as it bends right, with a wall to the left. In $1/4$ mile the path leaves the wall and you bear right to a stile. Cross the field to a gate at a road.

② At the road, turn left. After 400 yards look out for the 30mph signs.

③ Turn right at the footpath post just after the speed signs, onto a wide track. After 70 yards, take the path to the left. Then go through a gate into open pasture. There is no path visible in the field. Turn immediately right, going slightly uphill and keeping the wall to your right. At the top of the field, go through the gate, in the middle of the wall ahead. Then walk diagonally left uphill, to a signpost. Go over the stile, and take the path signed left, following the path to the right-hand side of a wall.

④ At the next wall, go over the stile and turn right, following the wall, slightly uphill. Go over a stile and continue with the wall to your right. Go over another stile. In a few yards is a footpath sign, at a wire fence. Bear slightly left, following the pointer across the field to the road.

⑤ Turn right and follow the road for just over $1/2$ a mile, to a gate.

⑥ Turn right at the footpath sign, over a stile, bear left uphill and over a stile. The path goes through three gates as it passes above Bank Wood. At the end of the wood, go through a gate and turn left, to reach a road.

⑦ Turn left and in a few yards turn right onto a footpath through Bramley Wood. Towards the end of the woods, pass through a rhododendron 'tunnel', and then descend gradually to a footpath sign.

⑧ Turn left at the sign and descend steeply. At the bottom, go over a stile, into a hollow and straight on up to a corner of a wire fence and wall. Go straight on for 115 yards, the wall to your right, towards a house.

⑨ At the footpath sign turn right, through a gate. In 15 yards turn right downhill, then ignore a path to the left. Go through a stile, keeping the wall to the left. Then go through a stile onto a lane. Turn right, to a road junction. Turn right, following the pavement to the main road, ignoring any side roads. Turn right, and take care crossing opposite the craft centre. Turn right, back over the footbridge, to the parking locations.

Walk 20 ~ White Edge and Froggatt Edge

Start: Curbar Gap, pay-and-display car park. **GR:** SK26257470.

Map: OS Exp. OL24. **Distance:** 6 miles (9.6 km). **Allow:** 3 hours.

Terrain: Generally good paths along the edges, but occasional muddy sections. Paths over fields.

Refreshments: The Grouse Inn, on the B6054.

Summary of the Walk: From the Curbar Gap car park, the walk gains height to reach White Edge. As you walk northwards along the edge, the views improve and include Kinder Scout and Mam Tor to the north-west. After descending to Froggatt Edge and Curbar Edge, the great views continue making this one of the most scenic walks in Derbyshire. August is a particularly good time to do the walk to see the heather in bloom.

Disadvantages: There are two road crossings. One or two fairly steep, but short sections. White Edge can sometimes be midgy on windless summer days.

Grading: Moderate. **Ascent:** 560ft (170m). **Max. height:** 1213ft (370m).

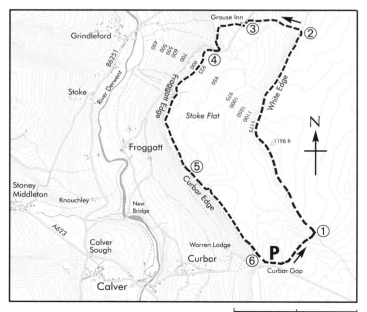

Directions

Go through the gate to the left-hand side of the car park entrance. (As seen from the car park). In 120 yards the path leaves the wall to continue straight on, descending to cross a footbridge in $1/3$ mile. You then walk uphill to a footpath junction and signpost.

① Turn left, signed 'White Edge' and follow the obvious path leading towards White Edge. In about $1/2$ mile you pass to the left of a trig. point (1198ft.) as you progress along the edge. After a further $1 1/2$ miles of walking along White Edge, there is a gap in a wall and a footpath sign.

② Turn left, signed 'Grouse Inn', walking downhill with a wall to your left. In $1/4$ mile there is a steeper rockier section. At the bottom ignore the bridleway signed to the right, keep straight on downhill through a wooded section. In 150 yards go through a gate and turn right, walking down a field towards buildings ahead. (The small boggy area is best crossed at the right-hand side). In 300 yards you come to a gate at the main road.

③ Go through the gate and turn left, crossing the main road opposite the Grouse Inn. Just after the pub, turn right going over the stile, signed 'footpath' and bear left down fields. In 320 yards go through a gate and turn left, passing a car park to your left. Ignore the path to the right and continue straight on. The path descends steeply to cross a stream and climbs up to a road. Go through the gate and turn right and cross the road in a few yards.

④ Go through the gate to the left onto a wide path gaining height slightly and going through wooded area. In about $1/2$ mile go through a gate and straight on. In a further $1/2$ mile ignore a path signed sharp right. In 380 yards is a post marked with an arrow. The wide path veers left*.

⑤ Go straight on following the arrow on a more scenic path gaining height along Curbar Edge. (*You can just keep on the wide path if you wish). In 350 yards bear right at a junction and in a further 105 yards you regain the wide path. Turn right and in $3/4$ mile you reach a gate across the track.

⑥ Go through the gate and keep straight on, ignoring the path going downhill to the right. In 160 yards, turn right down a few steps into the car park.

Walk 21 ~ Birchen Edge

Start: Birchen Edge car park (Free). Robin Hood. Off the A619.
GR: SK28107210.
Map: OS Exp. OL24. **Distance:** 3 1/2 miles (5.6 km). **Allow:** 2 hours.
Terrain: Good paths along the edges. Some marshy ground. Grassland.
Public toilets: None.
Refreshments: The Robin Hood Inn, adjacent to the starting point.
Summary: The walk quickly gains height giving good views as you walk along Birchen Edge. The rocks, known as 'The Three Ships' are a point of interest as is Nelson's Monument. Leaving the edge, the route crosses an area of boggy moorland, before returning along Gardom's Edge. Although close to Baslow, parts of this walk have an isolated atmosphere.
Disadvantages: A steep ascent onto Birchen Edge, and a boggy area of moorland, between points 3 and 4. Don't let this put you off though, because you can avoid the worst of the wet areas.
Grading: Moderate. **Ascent:** 425ft (129m). **Max. height:** 1017ft (310m).

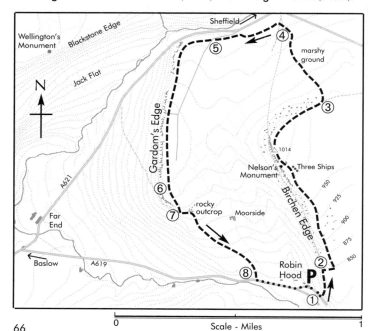

66

Scale - Miles

0   1

Turn left out of the car park entrance and follow the road for 65 yards. Then leave the road and turn left up to the gate and footpath sign.

1. Go through the gate onto the sandy path. After 220 yards there is a hawthorn tree and a prominent rock (inscribed ABL 10.07) on the left.

2. Turn right at the rock, going up a steep stony track. At the top, turn left on the narrow path, along Birchen's Edge. After half a mile you will come to three big rocks on your right. (Known as the 'Three Ships' and named after Nelson's flagships - 'Defiance', 'Victory' and 'Royal Soverin'). To the left is a stone column dedicated to Nelson's victory of the Battle of Trafalgar in 1805. Continue on the path, reaching a trig. point in 177 yards.

3. Keep straight on, along the level path following the edge. In about $1/4$ mile it bears left, descending to the moor. This area is sometimes wet, but the path avoids the worst of the boggy areas. In just under $1/2$ mile you reach a junction with a wider well-used path.

4. At the junction, go straight on over rough grass and after about 25 yards turn left at the junction with a well-defined grassy path. In $1/4$ mile the path reaches a fence. Walking with the fence to your right for 90 yards brings you to a fence corner and a gate.

5. Go through the gate and follow the narrow grassy path as it winds through birch trees, towards Gardom's Edge. Follow the sometimes indistinct grassy path alongside the edge. In 500 yards, go through a gap in the broken wall (ignoring the gate to the left) and continue along the edge. In another 560 yards another wall crosses the path.

6. Go through the gap in the wall and ignore the open gate, 60 yards on the left. Continue with the wall to your left as it bends to the right, down-hill, reaching a path junction at a large, shallow rock.

7. Turn left, going through the open gate. There are paths criss-crossing this area, but bear left going towards a distinctive rocky outcrop. Leave the rocks, bearing slightly right and downhill following a path through bracken. This joins a wider, grassy path descending slightly right towards the road near a wall corner.

8. Go over the stile and turn left, following the pavement back to the Robin Hood pub and the car park, just beyond.

Walk 22 ~ Chatsworth Park and Dobb Edge

Start: Nether End car park, Baslow. Pay-and-display. **GR:** SK25837214.
Map: OS Exp. OL24. **Distance:** 4½ miles (6.4 km). **Allow:** 2½ hours.
Terrain: Almost all of the walk is in the Chatsworth Estate. Surfaced tracks, and paths over grassland.
Public toilets: At the car park in Baslow and at Chatsworth House (during House opening hours only. House closed December 23rd - Easter).
Refreshments: Pubs in Baslow. Café and restaurant at Chatsworth House.
Summary: From Baslow the walk goes through Chatsworth Park, briefly following the river, then gaining height as it passes Chatsworth House. A quiet shaded road takes you behind the House, and then an enchanting path winds its way up past an ornamental aqueduct, with cascades and great views down to the House and gardens. A track then leads to the Hunting Tower, again with impressive views over the park and beyond. The final section crosses the northern end of the park, to regain Baslow.
Disadvantages: A fairly steep ascent up to the aqueduct, with steps.
Grading: Easy. **Ascent:** 430ft (131m). **Max. height:** 770ft (235m).

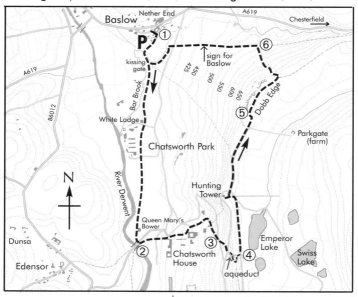

Directions

Turn right out of the car park and go straight on, over the bridge.

① After the bridge turn right, signed 'Chatsworth' going past a row of thatched cottages. At the end of the track in 250 yards, go through the Cannon Kissing Gate into Chatsworth Park. Ignore the footpaths signed to the left and keep straight on, along the wide track. After passing White Lodge in $1/3$ mile, continue straight on. In 330 yards go straight on at a crossroads. In just under $1/2$ mile, you reach a building, Queen Mary's Bower. Go straight on, through a gate to the road at a bridge.

② Cross the road and bear left on a wide gravel path. Go through a gate, and straight on at a crossroads to reach the House frontage. Go diagonally left and then bear right, walking up a wide straight road towards an imposing building. At the entrance turn left, signed 'Farmyard' and walk alongside the building. At its corner, go diagonally right to a road. Turn right, signed 'Farmyard and Playground' and go through a gate, by a cattle grid. In 50 yards on the left, ignore the road to the Farmyard.

③ In 280 yards, turn left on a path signed, 'The Dell'. In 120 yards keep straight on at a path crossroads to a road. Cross over onto a path. The path winds uphill to the top of the aqueduct. Don't go up the steps, but turn right, winding to the top of a waterfall. Then turn right for 4 yards.

④ Turn left on the wide track, (ignore a track right in 70 yards) and in $1/3$ mile, turn left at a junction. In 50 yards turn left at a telegraph post, and walk to The Hunting Tower. Retrace steps for 20 yards and turn left on wide path. In 45 yards, go straight on at a crossroads, signed 'Robin Hood'. In $1/3$ mile go straight on, where the tarmac road bends right. In 150 yards the path bends left, and in 25 yards you turn right over a stile.

⑤ Turn right and follow the path by the wall. In just under $1/3$ mile you reach a stile. Don't cross the wall, turn left on a path going downhill. In 85 yards at a fork, bear right. In 70 yards descend a path by the wall.

⑥ In 230 yards turn left, (when level with a gate). Follow a grassy track downhill. In just over $1/4$ mile go over a stile, signed 'Baslow'. Cross a gravel road and go straight on in the direction of the arrow on the sign (there is no defined path). In 300 yards cross a road and go straight on to a fence. Turn left following a path by the fence. In about 250 yards is the kissing gate. Go through the gate and retrace steps to the car park.

Walk 23 ~ Chatsworth Park and Edensor

Start: Calton Lees car park. Charge, most of the year. **GR:** SK25906855.
Map: OS Exp. OL24. **Distance:** 4¼ miles (6.8 km). **Allow:** 2½ hours.
Terrain: Private road, pasture, riverside paths.
Public toilets: None.
Refreshments: Café at Chatsworth Garden Centre, café at Edensor (at the Post Office, near the church).
Summary of the Walk: A gentle walk giving great views of Chatsworth Park. From Calton Lees the route gains height passing Calton Houses and then descends parkland to Edensor village. Every house is individually designed with a distinctive Swiss influence. The final section follows the meandering River Derwent with views across to Chatsworth House.
Disadvantages: At the start of the walk, the right of way follows a private road to Calton Houses. However, It is very lightly used by traffic.
Grading: Easy. **Ascent:** 450ft (137m). **Max. height:** 750ft (229m).

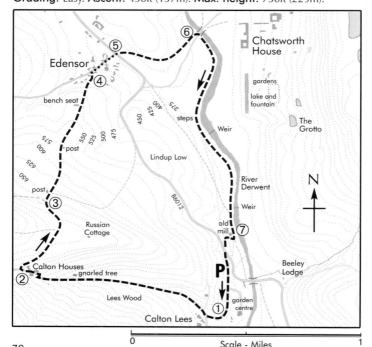

Directions

Leave the Calton Lees car park and turn right alongside the estate road (away from the main B6012 road). Ignore the road to the left (this goes to the garden centre). In about 400 yards, in Calton Lees village, ignore the road to the left (signed Rowsley).

① Go straight on at the bridleway sign, along the private road. It winds uphill for 4/5 mile to Calton Houses. After passing the last cottage, continue uphill for a short distance to a gate.

② Go through a gate, then turn right to follow a signed bridleway, running uphill, initially alongside a wall. At a crossroads in the open field, go straight on, following the sign 'Edensor, Chatsworth'. The building across to the right is called Russian Cottage. Go through another gate onto a wide, walled track, downhill through woods.

③ At the end of the track go through another gate on to open pasture, with great views over Chatsworth Park. Turn right going downhill heading for a guide post. Keep straight on ignoring the bridleway signed to the right, continuing downhill towards the left hand side of a copse. At the end of the second fenced copse, there is another guide post. The field levels off and the path becomes indistinct. Walk initially towards Edensor church spire, and then to the bench seat, situated beneath a prominent tree. From the seat walk straight on, you'll soon see a guide post, at which you bear right towards steps and an iron gate. (This is just to the right of a little sub-station).

④ Go up the steps and through the gate, and then down a steep flight of steps to the road. Turn right through the beautiful village of Edensor. At the village green, keep to the left hand side to reach the main gates.

⑤ Go through the swing gate and cross the main road (take care) to the wide, surfaced path, running diagonally right through Chatsworth Park. In 1/3 mile the path comes to the estate road, just before the bridge.

⑥ Cross the road, and walk beside the river. In 450 yards, go up the flight of steps and continue on the path by the river. Ignore any paths that leave the river. In 1/2 mile, you'll pass to the left of a ruined mill.

⑦ After the building turn sharp right, up the hill, to reach the road. (Ignore the diagonally left slanting path). Cross the road near the cattle grid and go through the gate, back to Calton Lees car park.

Walk 24 ~ Chatsworth Park and Swiss Lake

Start: Calton Lees car park. Charge, most of the year. **GR:** SK25906855.
Map: OS Exp. OL24. **Distance:** 5 ½ miles (8.8 km). **Allow:** 3 hours.
Terrain: Riverside path, Estate roads and field paths.
Public toilets: At Chatsworth House, during opening hours only.
Refreshments: Café at Chatsworth garden centre (near the start). Café and restaurant at Chatsworth House.
Summary of the Walk: After a pleasant riverside section, the route follows an estate road as it ascends through woodland to the viewpoint at the Hunting Tower. A track leads past Emperor Lake and Swiss Lake, before reaching the edge of Beeley Moor. There are good views to the south. The final section follows a farm lane back to the main road and the car park.
Disadvantages: A very short road section at the end of the walk, but care is needed as there is no pavement.
Grading: Easy. **Ascent:** 640ft (195m). **Maximum height:** 850ft (259m).

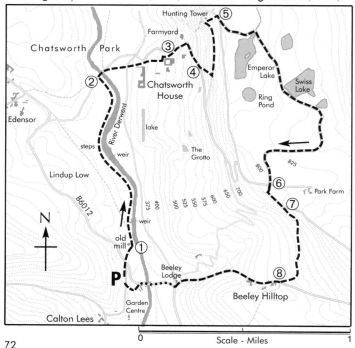

Directions

From the car park, return to the main road on the path running along-side it. Go through a gate and cross over adjacent to a cattle grid. Go down the steps and follow the path downhill to the old mill.

① Turn left and follow the riverside path passing a weir, and in $1/3$ mile a second weir is passed. After a further $1/2$ mile by the riverside the road is reached at a beautiful arched bridge.

② Turn right, cross the bridge and immediately bear right onto a wide path. Go through a gate and follow the path up towards Chatsworth House. At the House, bear slightly diagonally left across the frontage and then bear right, walking up the wide straight road towards an imposing building. At the entrance, turn left, signed 'Farmyard' and walk alongside the building. At its corner, go diagonally right to a road.

③ Turn right, signed 'Farmyard and Playground' and go through a gate, by a cattle grid. In 50 yards on the left, ignore the road to the Farmyard. Continue along the road as it bends right and upwards.

④ After about 280 yards, turn left on the footpath signed, 'The Dell'. Keep straight on at a path crossroads, up to a road. Turn left along the road which ascends gradually through woodland. In just over $1/3$ mile you emerge from the trees. In a few yards turn right up steps, to the Hunting Tower. Continue straight on passing to the right of the Tower. Follow a wide, straight, grassy clearing through trees to a junction.

⑤ Turn right on the shale road. In 50 yards ignore a path to the right. In about 300 yards you pass the first lake, Emperor Lake. Continue on the track and after $1/3$ mile you pass the more picturesque Swiss Lake. Continue past the lake and in $3/4$ mile you come to a crossroads.

⑥ Go straight on, signed 'Hob Hurst's House and Beeley'. Then in 150 yards, climb over the high stile and follow the track for 120 yards.

⑦ Turn right at the concessionary footpath sign, going diagonally downhill through bracken. At the end of the path, go over a stile and walk straight on, across a field towards a farm.

⑧ Go over a stile and turn right down the wide track. In just over $1/2$ mile you reach the main road at Beeley Lodge. Turn right along the road. Go over the bridge and cross the road. Turn left up the path, just before the bend, signed 'Footpath to Rowsley', back up to the car park.

Walk 25 ~ Stanton Moor

Start: Lay-by, along School Lane, Rowsley. **GR:** SK25686564.
Map: OS Exp. OL24. **Distance:** 6¼ miles (10Km). **Allow:** 3½ hours.
Terrain: Private road, field paths, moorland paths and short road sections.
Public toilets: None.
Refreshments: Cauldwell's Mill café, pub in Rowsley. (Not on the route).
Summary of the Walk: This walk includes the broad sweep of Darley Dale, interesting old quarried areas and the beautiful Stanton Moor. The route passes the ancient Nine Ladies Stone Circle. It is especially good in August for the heather in bloom on the moor.
Disadvantages: The right of way follows a private road at the start of the route. Be aware of occasional vehicles. A short, steep descent to the road between points 9 and 10.
Grading: Moderate. **Ascent:** 770ft (235m). **Max. height:** 1059ft (323m).

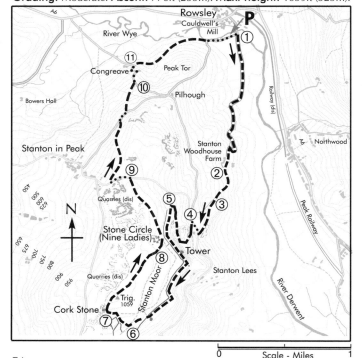

Leave the lay-by, walking back to the road corner near the bridge.

① Turn right along the road signed 'Private Road', and 'Public footpath to Stanton Lees'. In just under a mile at a bend, ignore the drive, signed 'Stanton Woodhouse. Private'. Keep on the road as it bends to the right and left, and walk past the buildings of Stanton Woodhouse Farm.

② Leave by the gate at the end of the farm and follow a wide grassy track. 60 yards after the stone gate posts, is a prominent rock to the left of the track. Bear left at this (an arrow is carved in it) up the field to a gate.

③ Go through the gate. The path skirts a disused quarry descending to a fork. Bear right to reach the road. Then turn right for about 100 yards.

④ Turn sharp left along a wide track. Follow the waymarked track, past a ruin, straight on, then bearing right up a wooded valley. In just under $1/4$ mile, the path bears left through trees, to reach a path junction at a wall.

⑤ Turn left, ignoring stiles to the right, reaching a tower in $1/3$ rd mile. Keeping a fence to your right, in 150 yards the path turns right, at the fence corner. In just under $1/2$ mile, is a large rock to the left of the path. To the right is a stile. Go over the stile and take the track to the left.

⑥ On reaching a broad sandy track at a slanting 'crossroads', go straight ahead on a narrow grassy path. This gains height and the route turns left on to a broad track. Ahead is the distinctively shaped Cork Stone.

⑦ Turn right at the stone and in 45 yards take the right-hand fork in the path, up to a trig. point. Continue straight on, to a wide sandy track.

⑧ Turn left and pass to the right of the Nine Ladies Stone Circle. Follow the wide track, straight on for just under $1/2$ mile to a road.

⑨ Turn left down the road and after 230 yards turn right, along a signed track. After passing a cricket ground, the path goes through woods, and descends steeply to a road. Turn right and after 170 yards, turn left at the stile, following a signed footpath diagonally right, downhill to a stile. Go straight on, heading for a stile, to the left of a gate, onto a lane.

⑩ Turn left, following the lane downhill for 280 yards to Congreave.

⑪ Turn right opposite Dovehouse Farm, on the signed path. Go through a gate and straight on, soon descending to cross a brook. Then go uphill and through a gate. Go straight on, keeping level until a line of big trees. A path then slants downhill, to the road. Turn left to the lay-by.

Walk 26 ~ Monyash and Bagshaw Dale

Start: Lay-by half a mile east of Monyash on B5055. **GR:** SK15756648.
Map: OS Exp. OL24.
Distance: 3 1/4 miles (5.2km). **Allow:** 2 hours.
Terrain: Paths along dales, field paths and a walled lane.
Public toilets: At the starting point.
Refreshments: Old Smith Café, and Bulls Head Inn, both in Monyash.
Summary of the Walk: This short walk starts from the head of Lathkill Dale. The route then gently gains height giving expansive views into the dale. A walled lane leads into the attractive village of Monyash. Several of the fields in this area are managed as meadows, and are covered in buttercups and other flowers around June. The final part of the walk follows Bagshaw Dale back to the lay-by.
Disadvantages: The walled lane leading into Monyash can be very muddy in winter, and Bagshaw Dale can be muddy at any time of the year.
Grading: Easy. **Ascent:** 220ft (68m). **Max. height:** 951ft (290m).

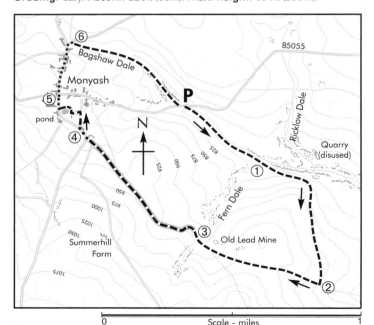

Directions

From the lay-by cross the road and go through the gate. Go straight on, along the broad dale. In about 300 yards go through a gate and after a similar distance go through another gate. In 55 yards, there is a metal gate and stile to the right of the path. (Another gate is just ahead).

① Go over the stile, leaving the dale path and follow the wide, grassy track as it gradually gains height, giving views into Lathkill Dale. It bears right towards the top, veering away from the wall. Stay on the obvious track, as it goes through a gate. Keep straight on until you reach a gate and a three-fingered signpost.

② Turn right (before the gate) signed Monyash, following the path uphill, along the right-hand side of a wall. At the top of the field, go over the stile, and turn right, following the Limestone Way sign, the wall to your right. At the end the field go through the gate, descending alongside the wall to go through another gate. The path then dips down and up as it crosses the head of Fern Dale.

③ Go through the gate, at the top of the rise. Turn left, the wall to your left and in 60 yards go through a gate onto a narrow, walled lane. After $1/2$ mile, go straight on at a junction with a narrow road. In a few yards, keep straight on, as this road joins a wider road. You are now in the attractive village of Monyash. After about 100 yards, a footpath is signed to the right.

④ Turn right at the sign, and in 90 yards turn left (just before reaching the church gate) along a narrow walled path. After passing the last building on the right, turn right and walk anticlockwise, halfway around the village pond, to join a road. Turn right along the road to reach the crossroads, by the village green, with its pub and café.

⑤ Go straight on at the crossroads, and after about 350 yards, turn right onto the road, signed Sheldon. After just 40 yards there is a stile and a footpath signed to the right. (Look carefully as It is obscured and set back from the road. It is opposite the sign to the left).

⑥ Turn right, going over the stile into Bagshaw Dale. Continue straight on along the dale, shortly going over a stile, then through a gate and over three more stiles. After going over the final stile, bear left and follow the wall back to the road, and the lay-by.

Walk 27 ~ Lathkill Dale (western section)

Start: Lay-by, or car park adjacent to toilet block, half a mile east of Monyash on B5055. **GR:** SK15756648.

Map: OS Exp. OL24. **Distance:** 4 ¾ miles (7.6km). **Allow:** 3 hours.

Terrain: Paths along the dale, a little rocky at the western end. One short section along a quiet lane. A narrow grassy path above Lathkill Dale. A stepped descent.

Public toilets: At the starting point.

Refreshments: None on route, but café and pub, both in Monyash.

Summary of the walk: The walk begins by descending into Lathkill Dale, a beautiful limestone valley, overlooked by high crags and interesting rock formations. The dale is noted for its plant life. In June you will see the rare Jacob's Ladder in flower. Leaving the dale, the route winds along an old lead mining track, up a secluded side valley to Haddon Grove. The final section follows an open access path above the dale, giving excellent views. It then descends steps alongside a disused quarry into the dale. The final part of the walk follows the outward route back to the road.

Disadvantages: Short, rocky section at the head of Lathkill Dale. A steep section of steps leading back down into the dale. The last part of the walk retraces outward steps, but only for ½ mile.

Grading: Moderate. **Ascent:** 480ft (146m). **Max. height:** 900ft (274m).

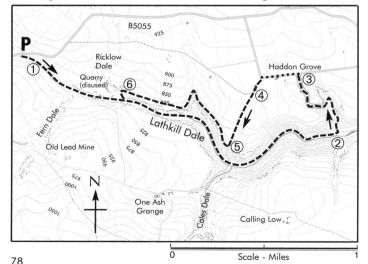

Go through the gate (on the same side of the road as the toilets). Go straight on, along the broad dale.

① In about 300 yards go through a gate and after a similar distance go through another gate. Then ignore the gate and stile to the right and go through the gate ahead. The route is initially rocky, you then go over a stile and the dale opens out to you. Continue straight on, along the dale and in $1/3$ mile note a cave to your right. *This is the source of the River Lathkill, but it is usually dry.* In just over $1/3$ mile you will pass a foot-bridge to your right. Then after about $1/4$ mile go through a gate and in 250 yards, over a stile. In $1/4$ mile you will pass an old mill pond and a shallow weir. A few yards further on there is a gate and a wall to its left. Do not go through the gate.

② Turn left, following the path up alongside the wall. The path soon broadens out into a wide track, winding its way purposely up and left, passing through two gates onto the level. Go straight on over a stile and continue past Mill Farm caravan site to your left, and on to a junction.

③ Turn left along the quiet road, until in 330 yards there is a sharp right-hand corner. Turn left along the drive of Haddon Grove Farm, signed public footpath. Keep straight on, passing just to the right of a building bearing a large 'Lathkill Dale' sign and straight on through the farm-yard. The last barn has a sign 'Lathkill Dale', arrowed 'straight on'.

④ Then go through the stile in a fence. A yellow arrow points straight ahead, ignore the one to the right. The path then goes through a gate, and crosses a camping field, to a stile almost opposite. Bear slightly right downhill and follow the path beside a wall. (There may be temporary tape fencing and stiles along here). When the wall ends, keep straight on down the field towards a gate, and the edge of Lathkill Dale.

⑤ Go through the gate and turn immediately right to follow a narrow path along the edge of the dale. It keeps a safe distance from the edge, more or less following a boundary wall. The views along and across the dale are excellent. In $3/4$ mile you come to a stile.

⑥ Go over the stile and in about 7 yards, turn sharp left down steps. These descend steeply alongside the disused Ricklow Quarry. At the bottom turn right, retracing outward steps for $1/2$ mile to the finishing point.

Walk 28 ~ Lathkill Dale (central section)

Start: Moor Lane, pay-and-display car park, or nearby lay-by.
GR: SK19406447.
Map: OS Exp. OL24. **Distance:** 5 ½ miles (8 km). **Allow:** 2 ¾ hours.
Terrain: Paths across fields. Steep descent into Cales Dale. Good, level path along Lathkill Dale, but a few rocky sections.
Refreshments: None on route. Pub in Over Haddon slightly off-route.
Summary of the Walk: This first part of the route goes over upland pastures, with excellent views, before descending into Cales Dale. This leads into Lathkill Dale, a steep-sided valley overlooked by impressive rock outcrops. It has some interesting remains of the lead mining industry, which flourished in the 18th and 19th centuries. The dale is important for wildlife, particularly plants, with many species that are nationally rare, including Jacob's Ladder and the Common Orchid. Leaving the dale the route gains height giving more views, passing through Meadow Place Grange, before crossing fields to reach a lane, and the parking area.
Disadvantages: The descent into Cales Dale is via steeply angled steps and rocky ledges that can be slippery. Meadow Place Grange can be muddy in winter. A section on a lane at the end (⅓ mile).
Grading: Moderate. **Ascent:** 450ft (137m). **Max. height:** 1000ft (305m).

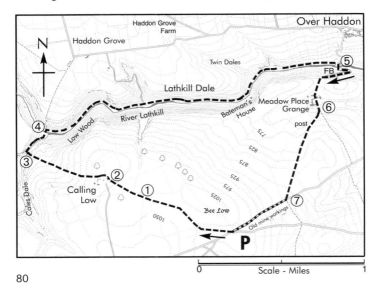

From the car park, turn left to the road junction and a lay-by. Cross the road and go through the stile, follow the path diagonally left to the stile at the farthest corner. In 35 yards diagonally right, go over another stile. Follow the path, bearing slightly left across a large field to a fence.

① Go through the gate and continue through a gate into Low Moor Wood. At the end of the woodland go through a gate. Walk diagonally left, heading initially towards the right-hand side of farm buildings. Before the farm entrance there is a gate and footpath signed to the right.

② Go through the gate and straight on to a gate in wall on the left. There is a quick succession of three gates as the path goes through woods. After the third gate, descend slightly right for 75 yards. Go through the gate, signed Cales Dale. Continue descending two more fields, going through three gates, the last one leading to the edge of Cales Dale. Go down the steps and over a stile, turning right, signed Lathkill Dale.

③ In 50 yards, turn right at the junction with a wider path and follow the stony path which joins Lathkill Dale at a footbridge.

④ Cross the bridge and turn right along the dale, after about 1/3 mile go through a gate, then in 250 yards, go over a stile. After 110 yards there is a small waterfall. In about 330 yards there are two gates in quick succession. In just over 1/2 mile, a footbridge gives an optional diversion to Bateman's House. After another 3/4 mile you reach a gate at a road. Bear right and follow the road down to the stone-slabbed bridge.

⑤ Go over the bridge and turn left, following the wide track as it winds up through woodland. At the top go through a gate and turn left, following a sign over a field. Go through two gates, then straight on over the farm courtyard, to the gate opposite (to the left a building). Climb the high stile and walk between walls to the sign at the right-hand wall corner.

⑥ Ignore the path signed left, but follow the wall to the right. In 40 yards bear left up the hill, signed from the wall 'Middleton'. Go past a wooden guide post and continue in the same direction to the stile in the wall ahead. Go over the stile, and follow the path to a stile at a field corner. Continue in the same direction across the next field to a stile at the road.

⑦ Go over the stile and turn right, following the road for about 1/3 mile to the lay-by. If parked at the car park, turn left at the junction.

Walk 29 ~ Lathkill Dale (eastern section)

Start: Lay-bys on both sides of the road in Alport. **GR:** SK27966456.
Map: OS Exp. OL24. **Distance:** 5 1/2 miles (8.8 km). **Allow:** 3 hours.
Terrain: Good paths along the dales. Paths over grassland and one muddy section at Meadow Place Grange.
Public toilets: None.
Refreshments: None on route, but pubs in Youlgrave and Over Haddon.
Summary of the Walk: From Alport the walk follows a crystal clear trout river along Bradford Dale. The route follows an old lead mining track out of the dale and gains height crossing fields towards Meadow Place Grange. There are panoramic views over the surrounding landscape before you descend into Lathkill Dale, following the beautiful riverside path along its eastern end back to Alport.
Disadvantages: Numerous step-stiles. The path near Meadow Place Grange can be very muddy.
Grading: Easy. **Ascent:** 550ft (167m). **Maximum height:** 867ft (264m).

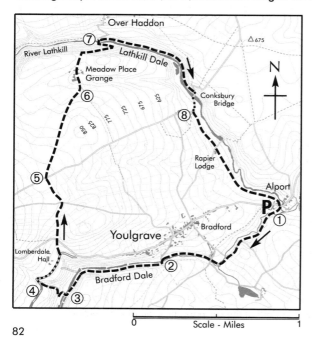

From the lay-by walk down the hill to the phone box and the river. Turn right at the phone box, signed 'footpath', along a tarmac track.

① Go through a gate, following the riverside path along Bradford Dale. In just under $1/2$ mile is a packhorse bridge. Don't cross it, keep straight on reaching a gate at a road in 220 yards. Go straight on for 40 yards, passing a stone slab footbridge to your left and go through a gate, to follow the riverside path. In just over $1/4$ mile is a gate.

② Go through a gate and turn left over a stone footbridge. Then turn right.

③ In $3/4$ mile turn right, crossing the river by a bridge. In 40 yards ignore a footpath to the right. Keep on the track as it winds gradually up and out of the dale. In just over $1/4$ mile you reach a road.

④ Go through the stile and turn right. In $1/4$ mile where the road bends right, cross over and go through the gate at the 'Limestone Way' sign. Walk straight on, up the field. Go up steps to the road and cross over. Go through a gate at a sign for 'Over Haddon'. The path goes uphill with a wall to the right, crossing several fields to reach a stile at a road after $1/4$ mile. Cross the road and go over the stile. Walk straight on crossing the field towards a line of trees. Go over a stile and in 30 yards over another stile. Walk up the field, go through a stile and cross a road.

⑤ Go over the stile and bear right, descending a large field. Go over a stile and continue descending in the same direction. Go over the next stile, walking in the same direction towards a farm below.

⑥ Keep the wall to your left, go through gate posts and between walls to a high stile. Go over the stile and follow the wide track, crossing the open farmyard to an entrance between buildings opposite. Walk between the buildings, signed 'Over Haddon'. Go up through a gate and bear slightly right, up the field. In 200 yards, go through a gate and descend a wide track reaching a slabbed footbridge in about 300 yards.

⑦ Go over the bridge and turn right along the popular riverside path. In $3/4$ mile turn right at a road, descending to go over Conksbury Bridge.

⑧ In 90 yards turn left at a gap in the wall, signed 'footpath'. In $1/4$ mile cross a lane and go straight on, past Rapier Lodge. Keep straight on through every stile and gate and in just over $1/2$ mile you reach the road at Alport. Turn right up the road back to the lay-bys.

Walk 30 ~ Robin Hood's Stride

Start: On Main Street, Elton, just after Back Lane. **GR:** SK22476094.
Map: OS Exp. OL24. **Distance:** 2 ¾ miles (4.4km). **Allow:** 1½ hours.
Terrain: Field paths, lanes, gravel tracks.
Public toilets: None. **Refreshments:** Pub and café in Elton. The Duke of York is a joyous rarity. (Open evenings and Sunday lunchtime).
Summary: A short, but interesting walk from the village of Elton. You descend a quiet lane, before gaining height to reach the twin rocks (Weasel and Inaccessible Pinnacles), known as Robin Hood's Stride. Another point of interest is Hermit's Cave. This isn't on the route, but to see it go through the gate to the right of Hilary's Seat, (see text) go up and then right through the woods and search around for the cave. From the Stride the route follows an open access path to a lane and across fields to Elton.
Disadvantages: Two sections on lanes, but they are both lightly used by traffic. A muddy section churned by cows near the start of the route.
Grading: Easy. **Ascent:** 460ft (140m). **Maximum height:** 900ft (274m).

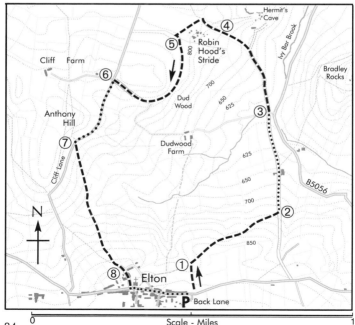

Directions

From the suggested parking area, cross the road and walk away from the village, going about 40 yards past the Back Lane junction. Turn left at the footpath sign, going over a stile and following a stony track, to the left-hand side of a playing field. In 300 yards, go over a stile and walk straight on for 10 yards (until level with a telegraph pole to your left).

① Then turn right onto a narrow grassy path. The path descends to the right of trees, into a muddy hollow. (The worst of the mud can be avoided by looping to the right). At the end of the trees continue straight on, descending the field gently, to reach a lane.

② Go over a stile, and turn left down the lane. In $1/3$ mile you cross a track.

③ Go straight on through a gate at the 'Limestone Way' sign. Follow the gravel track uphill. In 350 yards the track bends right and you continue straight on, along a grassy path. (In 200 yards is 'Hilary's Seat').

④ Go through a gate and uphill on the stony track, in 140 yards, turn left over a stile at a wire fence, signed 'Limestone Way'. Bear slightly left, away from the wall, ignoring the stile to the right. The path gains a little height, passing to the right of the rocky jumble of Robin Hood's Stride. When level with the second pinnacle, ignore the path to the right, go straight on descending to a wall, with a narrow stile. Don't go through the stile, turn left passing between a stone gatepost and a tree. Walk with the wall to your right for 40 yards, until you reach a gate.

⑤ Turn right, going through the gate at an 'open access' sign. Keep straight on and in 200 yards is a farm gate to the left. Don't go through this but bear right, continuing on a narrow path. In 250 yards you go over a stile and the path bears right, joining a farm track, just above a barn. Turn right along the track, reaching a road junction in 200 yards.

⑥ At the road junction turn left and in $1/4$ mile there is a stile on the left.

⑦ Turn left, going through the stile and straight on down a field. The path goes through two gates and a stile. After the stile, continue straight on crossing a hollow. The path then bears slightly right uphill to a stone stile. It then continues uphill reaching a wall and sign at the top of the hill.

⑧ Turn left and go through a gate, turn right on a track. In 70 yards, bear right on a lane. Turn left at the main road, passing the church and the pub. In $1/4$ mile you will regain the suggested parking area.

Elevation Profiles - walks 1 - 8

Walk 1 - Bretton Clough & Abney

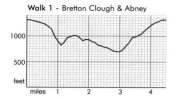

Walk 2 - Eyam Moor and Stoke Ford

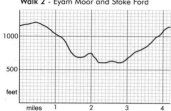

Walk 3 - Eyam and Riley Graves

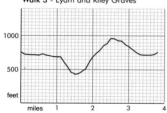

Walk 4 - Padley Gorge

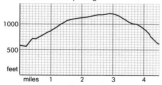

Walk 5 - Longshaw Estate

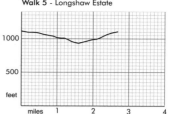

Walk 6 - Chee Dale

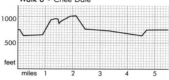

Walk 7 - Monk's Dale

Walk 8 - Tideswell Dale

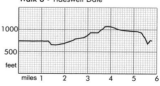

Elevation Profiles - walks 9 - 17

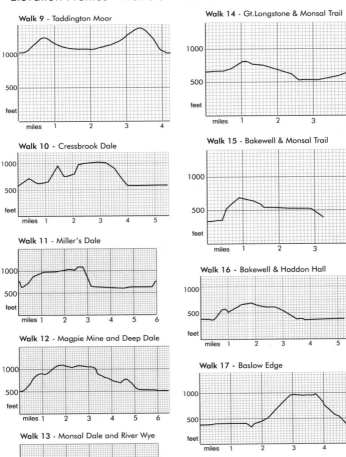

Walk 9 - Taddington Moor

Walk 10 - Cressbrook Dale

Walk 11 - Miller's Dale

Walk 12 - Magpie Mine and Deep Dale

Walk 13 - Monsal Dale and River Wye

Walk 14 - Gt.Longstone & Monsal Trail

Walk 15 - Bakewell & Monsal Trail

Walk 16 - Bakewell & Haddon Hall

Walk 17 - Baslow Edge

Elevation Profiles - walks 18 - 26

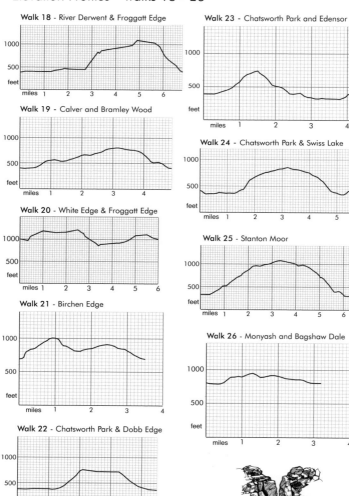

Walk 18 - River Derwent & Froggatt Edge

Walk 19 - Calver and Bramley Wood

Walk 20 - White Edge & Froggatt Edge

Walk 21 - Birchen Edge

Walk 22 - Chatsworth Park & Dobb Edge

Walk 23 - Chatsworth Park and Edensor

Walk 24 - Chatsworth Park & Swiss Lake

Walk 25 - Stanton Moor

Walk 26 - Monyash and Bagshaw Dale

Elevation Profiles - walks 27 - 30

Walk 27-Lathkill Dale - western section

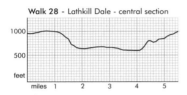

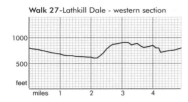

Sheepwash Bridge,
Ashford in the Water

Walk 28 - Lathkill Dale - central section

Rutland Hotel, Bakewell

Walk 29- Latkill Dale - eastern section

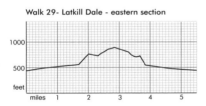

Tea Rooms, Eyam

Walk 30 - Robin Hood's Stride

Red Lion, Litton

Useful Addresses

Peak District National Park Authority
Aldern House
Baslow Road
Bakewell DE45 1AE
Tel: 01629 816200
web: www.peakdistrict.org
email: customer.service@peakdistrict.gov.uk

Youth Hostels Association (YHA)
Trevelyan House
Dimple Road
Matlock
Derbyshire DE4 3YH
Tel: 01629 592600
web: www.yha.org.uk

Ramblers' Association
2nd Floor
Camelford House
87-90 Albert Embankment
London SE1 7TW
Tel 020 7339 8500
web: www.ramblers.org

Tourist Information Centre
Old Market Hall
Bridge Street
Bakewell DE45 1DS
Tel: 01629 813227
Email: bakewell@peakdistrict-npa.gov.uk

Reporting path problems:
Derbyshire County Council (Highways Authority)
County Hall
Matlock
DE4 3AG
Tel 0845 6058058 or 01629 736200
website: www.derbyshire.gov.uk
email: contact.centre@derbyshire.gov.uk

Bibliography

Below is a list of Peak District and Derbyshire related books that may be of interest. The date given is the year of first publication. Many are out of print, but you may be able to find copies at - www.abebooks.com or www.amazon.co.uk. (also at real bookshops).

The Best of the Sheffield Clarion Ramblers' Handbook - Ward's Piece, Edited by David Sissons. Halsgrove 2002.

Byways, Boots and Blisters, Bill Laws. Sutton Publishing 2008.

Derbyshire in the Civil War, Brian Stone. Scarthin Books 1992.

East Midlands and The Peak, Edited by G Grigson. Collins 1951.

First and Last, Roland Smith. Peak Park Joint Planning Board 1978.

Freedom to Roam, Howard Hill. Moorland 1980.

Geology Explained in the Peak District, FW Cope. Scarthin Books 1988.

The Guide Stoops of the Dark Peak, H Smith. H Smith 1999

Hanged for a Sheep - Crime in bygone Derbyshire, EG Power. Scarthin Books 1988.

Highways and Byways in Derbyshire, JB Frith. MacMillan & Co. 1905.

Kinder Scout, Edited by Roly Smith. Various publishers 2002.

Lead Mining in the Peak District, Peak District Mines Historical Society. Peak Park Joint Planning Board 1968.

Moors, Crags and Caves of the High Peak, EA Baker. Heywood 1903 (reprinted by Halsgrove, 2002.)

Mountain Rescue - History and Development in the Peak District, Ian Hurst, Roger Bennet. Tempus Publishing 2007.

Odd Corners in Derbyshire, William Palmer. Skeffington & Son 1938.

The Peak and Pennines, WA Poucher. Constable 1966.

The Peak District Café Guide, A McCloy, Johnson Publishing 2003.

The Peak District Pub Guide, A McCloy, Johnson Publishing 2002.

Peakland Lead Mines and Miners, HM Parker. Moorland 1979.

Peakland Pubs - A Pint-Sized History, Andrew McCloy. Halsgrove 2005.

The Peak District - Pictures from the Past, L Porter. Moorland 1984.

Peak District Place Names, Martin Spray. John N Merrill 1989

It Could Be a Little Gold Mine - Tales of a Derbyshire Innkeeper, David Allingham. Illustrations by Bill Tidy. Johnson Publishing 2005 (Available from Johnson Publishing £5.00 inc. postage).

Index of main features (numbers refer to walk numbers)

Index

The End